"*A New Vision for Early Childhood* gives us a compelling understanding of who children are, what they need from parents and teachers, and what they are capable of. And here's some relieving news for parents: We can stop hovering. We can do less. We can trust more."

Dr. Becky Kennedy, CEO & Founder, Good Inside.

"Deeply personal and richly detailed, Hichenberg's illuminating exploration of a child's life is essential reading for parents, educators, and all those eager to understand the troubling experience of young children today."

Dr. Paula S. Fass, author: *The End of American Childhood: A History of Parenting from Life on the Frontier to the Managed Child*

"*A New Vision* reframes the toddler world so we can radically reframe our relationships with young children and let go of adult-driven control. An eye-opening book every parent and educator must read."

Dr. Tovah P. Klein, author: *Raising Resilience; How Toddlers Thrive;* Director, Barnard Center for Toddler Development

"Using cutting-edge approaches to human development, Hichenberg lays out profoundly novel perspectives about young children. *A New Vision* is about the urgent need to challenge our faulty notions about children, parenting, and ultimately, ourselves. Written in an accessible way, the book speaks to a vast audience of scholars, parents, teachers, and de facto all adults."

Dr. Anna Stetsenko, author: *The Transformative Mind;* Psychology professor, CUNY Graduate Center

"In vivid detail, Hichenberg shows how our expectations of young children actually diminish their remarkable capacities and competencies. *A New Vision* artfully recasts their resistance to our expectations as their need to explore, to be set free, to find their way in this world."

Dava Schub, CEO & Museum Director, Children's Museum of Manhattan

A New Vision for Early Childhood

This innovative and thought-provoking book invites you to move away from strategies of control and toward relationships of trust with young children. This book presents the conceptual foundation for this re-framed relationship as well as pragmatic takeaways for parents and teachers of preschool-aged children. The book offers a concise, critical history of early childhood which is then laid against the author's ethnographic research into the daily life of one 2-year-old. This unique and refreshing perspective offers intimate insight into the tension between the adult's desire for control and the child's capacity for resistance. The author argues that when the adult-child relationship is defined by control, the child is faced with the same choice on repeat: submit, or resist. Taking action in accordance with personal wants and needs typically requires transgressing adult expectations. For the child, in today's hyper-surveilled childhood, to speak up is to resist. Moving these ideas from research and theory back into preschools and homes, *A New Vision for Early Childhood* is important reading for any preschool teacher, leader, or parent who wants to reconsider their relationship with children. We can become allies instead of sheriffs, working with children instead of against them.

Noah Hichenberg is a preschool director and former classroom teacher in Washington, DC, and an adjunct professor at the American Jewish University's School of Educational Leadership. He received his Ed.D. from Teachers College, Columbia University, in curriculum and teaching with a focus in early childhood.

A New Vision for Early Childhood

Rethinking Our Relationships with Young Children

Noah Hichenberg

Routledge
Taylor & Francis Group

NEW YORK AND LONDON

Designed cover image: © Noah Hichenberg

First published 2025
by Routledge
605 Third Avenue, New York, NY 10158

and by Routledge
4 Park Square, Milton Park, Abingdon, Oxon, OX14 4RN

Routledge is an imprint of the Taylor & Francis Group, an informa business

© 2025 Taylor & Francis

ISBN: 978-1-032-59706-5 (hbk)
ISBN: 978-1-032-57702-9 (pbk)
ISBN: 978-1-003-45592-9 (ebk)

DOI: 10.4324/9781003455929

Typeset in Palatino
by KnowledgeWorks Global Ltd.

Contents

Meet the Author

Noah Hichenberg has spent the past 12 years as a preschool director, first in New York City and now in Washington, DC, and was previously a teacher in 3-year-old classrooms for 5 years. Noah received his Masters in Early Childhood and Childhood Education from Fordham University and earned his Doctor of Education degree in Curriculum and Teaching with an focus in early childhood at Teachers College, Columbia University. For his dissertation he spent nine months shadowing a two-year-old child throughout their daily life, from which he developed novel and critical insights into how children experience the social construction of early childhood. His work continually focuses on the transformative power of a young child's agency in the face of adult expectations. Noah has hosted regular Coffee Chats for preschool parents for several years as well as written a weekly newsletter, Noah's Notes, about preschool, parenting, and community; Noah's ongoing writing is available on the Substack handle @noahhichenberg. Noah currently serves as an adjunct professor at the American Jewish University, where he teaches a graduate class on current research trends in early childhood. He has led and taught at workshops and conferences on a variety of topics. Noah lives in Maryland with his wife and four children.

Introduction

There is a secret underlife in a preschool and the various spaces of early childhood – children's powerful ideas. They run rampant, each one a vibrant Neverland, waiting to be mapped, explored, populated, and illustrated. They are already there, before you even look for them – a brimming multiverse of Neverlands, ongoing and present despite our blindness to them, our propensity to hurry our children along, and our insistence they leave their fantasy behind. We need only to stop teaching and stop parenting to see them flourish in front of us, to see our children bring their ideas to life. Young children are constantly engaged in creating dynamic, meaningful relationships with each other, with the world, and with their ideas. They ceaselessly generate prosperous and substantive imaginary landscapes. Disconnected from the teachers' curriculum, far afield from the parents' expectations, these Neverlands exist within the child's culture, generated from within and appearing strange and unknown from the outside. Their ideas are constantly evolving, reciprocating, and mushrooming. The young child's thoughts slide around easily and fluidly within this social under-life, exchanged in the open with playmates, given away eagerly and consumed greedily, only to be given back yet again, returned polished and shined, expanded and extended. Rich and fertile, these gemstones are the child's aspirations and hopes – the things they cherish most, the things they so desire, their novel gifts to the world.

And then we – their teachers and parents, those clinging to control – tell them to stop. It is time to move on. We're running late, find your shoes. Hurry up. Why won't you listen? We're leaving. Where are your shoes!

This book presents a vision for rethinking our relationships with young children by exploring how and why adults attempt to control the daily lives of young children, what is lost when we do so, and how adults can cede ground back to children. Young children come to matter in the world through their ceaseless production of novel ideas and their powerful desire to have a say in their life. This happens in small, local ways, often missed by adults as we rush children through their life, insisting they behave appropriately, according to our predetermined cultural expectations for a child their age. The young child must push back against these adult expectations and instructions in order to have their say and to express their ideas. They come to matter *through their resistance:* in relationships oriented around control, the child is defined through either compliance or resistance.

I tell this story from a personal standpoint, weaving together my experiences as a preschool teacher, preschool director, doctoral student, childhood researcher, education professor, and, oh, I should mention, a parent of four children. My wife and I welcomed our first born in my first year as a school director, our second came three years later (born on Trump's inauguration day), and our pandemic twins rounded out the family in summer 2020. My writing is peppered with examples from the lives of young children and their families I have met in the field along the way, woven together with inspiration from a wide range of thinkers, authors, and academics.

Here is a new vision for our relationship with young children, described through a unique, critical exploration of early childhood education and preschool-aged children, with a focus on the tension between adult control and child agency. Children, as humans, *matter*: they are living, breathing, striving, creating. Parents and teachers try to control the child which diminishes their mattering. It is the intersection between these two phenomena into which I dive.

In Chapter 1, I begin by sharing the story of how I arrived at the questions and perspectives that led to this book along with descriptions of the current state of parenting and teaching young children. Chapter 2 offers a succinct, critical history of early childhood in the United States. I review the social and cultural construction of preschool and early childhood education – a specific history which had not yet been written – to reveal how the urge to control children came to be the overwhelmingly dominant feature of adult attitudes toward young children. In Chapter 3,

I share unique ethnographic research, offering an intimate portrait of contemporary early childhood through the daily life of one two-year-old, Emily, with a focus on control, resistance, and agency. There is no comparable existing body of research; to my knowledge, no one has spent this amount of time with a child this age, in this setting, with this lens. Chapter 4 presents a new vision for childhood, bringing in additional perspectives from my experiences as a preschool teacher and director. I outline a sought-after-future that I believe we can bring to life. Chapter 5 concludes by offering practical takeaways for parents and teachers as we rethink our relationship with young children. Ultimately, the book offers more questions than answers, more problems than solutions. I do not arrive at one truth – this is an invitation for exploration and critical thinking. I am curious where it will lead.

This call to arms asks us to reimagine preschool and early childhood as a space where we can *stop parenting* and *stop teaching*. We do not always need to be "on"! Children need space, away from adults! I urge adults to shift their relationships with young children so that we can look *across* at children instead of *down* at them, so that we can *listen more* and *hurry less*, so that we can give children the space and time needed to explore their many Neverlands.

This book is not about teaching or parenting – it is about not-teaching and not-parenting; it is about adults seeing what happens when they get out of the way. There are many times that adult control in a young child's life is necessary and helpful. This book is not about those times – this is not about *parenting advice* or *teaching strategies*. This is about building mutual, reciprocal relationships with children, oriented around seeing humanity in the other despite our desire to control them. It is a book about *knowing* children, not *changing* them. This is about how much adult control young children face throughout their daily life and how and where the parent or teacher can re-orient the relationship away from control as the defining feature. It is about how we can re-introduce ourselves to young children and re-imagine our relationship with them.

It is about allowing children to matter.

Noah Hichenberg

Foreword

"Grown-ups never understand anything by themselves, and it is tiresome for children to be always and forever explaining things to them" – these stunningly counter-intuitive words are from Antoine de Saint-Exupéry's novella *The Little Prince*, about childhood trial and tribulations yet also its creativity and discoveries, indeed its miracles and true magic. These words call on us to pause and think about who the little children actually are and who we are vis-à-vis them, challenging much of what appears to us to be self-evident. The fabulous book by Noah Hichenberg answers this important call. In essence, the book is about the urgent need for adults – all of us and, especially, parents and teachers – to see, hear, understand, acknowledge, respect, and value young children, including those who are just entering communal life and learning to be its members.

One could object that we do see and value children – indeed, how could we not as we parent and teach? Yet the point is about the need to do all of this much better and with much greater depth, awareness, and insight, in much more egalitarian and non-authoritarian ways, all while drastically changing our habitual ways of thinking about and interacting with children. The author succeeds in conveying this quite radical message, in a text written with great passion and conviction, while drawing on a diverse body of scholarship in support of the book's many important theoretical points all related to this core message. This, by itself, is no small feat since we still lack sufficient representations of ideas about young children's unsurpassed worth, infinite value, and inimitable rights for respect and acknowledgment.

Quite critically, the author also succeeds in demonstrating how exactly it is possible to change our parenting and teaching, as based in changing our very ideas about young children and ourselves – and does so in an accessible way that should speak to a vast audience of scholars, practitioners, parents, teachers, and de facto all adults. This is achieved by the author avoiding complicated language without losing the depth of ideas and, also, by drawing on his own vast experiences as a researcher, teacher, and parent. The most gripping parts of the book depict the story of Emily, a two-year-old, in her every day and seemingly routine interactions with the world, while the author is following her and looking closely and thinking deeply about what is going on. Along the way, centuries-old yet deeply faulty notions about children are questioned and challenged. In the process, the "big" theories of childhood, human development, sociocultural dynamics, and society at large all coalesce and come alive to reveal profound lessons about Emily, ourselves, and practically all of humanity.

For many readers, the core message about this radical change in perspective – implying that we need to learn to parent and teach anew, breaking with many traditions, stereotypes, and rules – might come as a surprise. Indeed, many of the leading frameworks in mainstream psychology and education (still heavily tainted by behaviorism and other mechanistic, top-down views) posit people as recipients of stimuli that are directly molding them in determining all developmental outcomes. That is, the dominant conceptions still prioritize unidirectional shaping of development, with children supposed to absorb external impacts, each as a solitary "achiever" on an individualized course into adulthood. Relatedly, human beings are seen as having practically no role in the process of development as they, essentially, *do not matter* – being shaped and molded by the outside world.

Yet there is a solid body of ideas developed through the past (at least) century that speak, if not scream, exactly about the urgency of changing this perspective and in his book Hichenberg sets on a journey to represent and advance these. Among others, he draws on Vygotsky's works that pioneered notions about the bidirectional, distributed, and reciprocal nature of human development. In this perspective, every step and outcome in human development is immersed in, and only comes about, as a dimension of shared pursuits, collaborative explorations, and joint experiences. In this sense, nothing of any significance happens for and to people, including children, in ways of one-sided, unidirectional influences and (especially) top-down impositions. Instead, we are closely entangled in relationships, so that we develop and learn always and only together, in back-and-forth exchanges and mutual collisions – all as give-and-take processes by their very nature.

Hichenberg draws on many radical theories and ideas that resonate with and expand on this perspective, which still remains marginalized and to a great extent novel though in fact its roots go back into at least the past century. Among others, he graciously and creatively draws on my works on Transformative Activist Stance that prioritize the notion that all people – each and every one of us, including very young children from the very moment of birth – inevitably participate in and, more critically, agentively contribute to all events and occurrences in life, *including their own development*. I maintain that human development is a process of an active interchange with the world through which people bring into existence (co-create, co-produce, co-realize) both themselves and their world – all in the dynamic flow of ceaseless back-and-forth transactions and exchanges between people and the world, in the process of their mutual and synchronous coming about. That is, the "external" world, on the one hand, and human development in all of its incarnations and outcomes, on the other, appear as co-arising, co-evolving – and, even more radically, co-realizing, each other, since they do not pre-exist each other. In other words, development comes about through fluid, bidirectional, conjoint, and continuous enactments that people, including even very young children, themselves carry out in shared spaces and collaborative pursuits. Development, therefore, does not just happen to people – it is a collaborative and creative accomplishment, a process that comes down to mutual work and effort within and through collective activities and their affordances and mediations, as well as obstacles and contradictions, as these are co-created by all people collaborating in together agentively enacting these very activities.

Thus, as we parent and teach children, we need to remember that it is a dual, or two-sided, back-and-forth interactional process that unfolds as the work and effort of both adults and children and in which, therefore, everything is subject to negotiation for it to be meaningful and successful. This is if by success we mean communal well-being and mutual flourishing in a world that is equitable and fair for all. Many of the authors the book draws upon speak – in various voices and words – to exactly this message. For example, consider Madeline Levine's powerful words that "If pushing, direction, motivation and reward always come from the outside, the child never has the opportunity to craft an inside."

I believe that after reading Hichenberg's book, we have a better chance to be further moved along the lines of radically new perspectives on childhood and humanity as a whole. He invites us to discover alternative ways to parent and teach and to learn those ways from children as we teach and parent. Presented throughout this book are novel ways of relating to young children, ways that are more sensitive, engaged, resonant, attuned, synergistic, understanding, and overall, more caring and respectful of children. His advice and specific guides for what he terms "horizontal parenting" are concrete, insightful, and extremely helpful, written as four "Stances" of Symmetry, Shedding, Listening, and Ceding. Together, these stances show how we can parent without disappearing from children's lives and instead be present in them as the child's companions, collaborators, and co-creators of our mutual lives and shared worlds.

And then again, childhood is truly about magic and miracles in its openness and infinite potential, as a reminder that the future can be different and better if we together work at it. The flourishing of agency, creativity, daring, and imagination in childhood, its ineliminable drive for freedom, such as shown by Emily – if only we open our eyes and attune ourselves to seeing and appreciating these – is a true treasure for all of humanity. The need for these miracles to be turned into reality is especially dire now, in our troubled times. Today, we need to be explained by children that the world seen through their eyes – as Noah Hichenberg helps us to appreciate – might actually be the way into a better future for us all.

Dr. Anna Stetsenko

1

Interrupting Neverland

The Outlaw and the Sheriff

"I know, I know. You don't want to, but you need to." Emily, two years old with a spunky ponytail and fading red nail polish, is dismayed at these instructions from her preschool teacher. It is time to clean up and Emily has already rejected the demand with a vehement, "No!" They are at a tense standstill – I imagine an outlaw and a sheriff in an old Western, hands on their hips as they face each other, poised to draw, a tumbleweed blowing by. Neither budge. I am the curious observer, peeking from behind a dusty saloon window, eyes wide. Emily stands tall despite her meager stature, her stubborn persistence bulking her up a bit. This tactic of hers, the only weapon in her arsenal, is well-honed from near-constant use. To me, spending the year shadowing her while conducting ethnographic research about being two, her life seems to be a daily encounter with a coordinated system of rules and expectations – there is always a sheriff. Emily's choice is to either submit or resist as she moves from adult to adult and place to place.

The young child's life is filled with this same choice, over and over and over again.

A persistent focus on control is an odd and ugly ingredient to be so readily present in so many human relationships. This desire – to control – has become ubiquitous and foundational

DOI: 10.4324/9781003455929-1

in how adults today see, understand, and relate to young children. A critical review of the relationship describes that:

> To treat someone like a child is, roughly, to treat her as if her life is not quite her own to lead and as if her choices are not quite her own to make. [In modern society] each person is a sovereign authority whose consent is not to be bypassed…. [and yet] we do not feel bound by children's expressions of their wills in the same way that we feel bound by adults' expression of theirs…
>
> Our basic concept of a child is that of a person who in some fundamental way is not yet developed, but who is in the process of developing. It is in virtue of children's undeveloped condition that we feel we have special obligations to them… [such as] duties to protect, nurture, discipline, and educate…. We think of children as people who have to be raised, whether they like it or not.
>
> Tamar Schapiro, 1999, pp. 715–717

Children's lives are not their own to lead. Rules and resistance, and the tension between them, are the daily topography Emily must navigate, the terrain she traverses. When Emily doesn't want to put her jacket on, her babysitter reminds her, "I know you don't want to, but…." In the hallway outside her class, her mother helps her prepare to enter for the morning by removing her boots and jacket. Here it comes, the familiar drumbeat of outlaw-meets-sheriff: "No! I don't want to!" followed by, "Sorry, that's the rule." When her request for a snack while being pushed in her stroller is denied by her mother, Emily is forceful and clear in her rebuttal: "I don't want you to say no I want you to say yes." I reflect with her mother about this line later that night, and she nods knowingly: "She says stuff like that all the time." All the time! She would later tell me this resistance is present "almost in *every single interaction*" (stressing those last three words), while her father chimed in to say the frequency was "off the charts."

This drumbeat is the soundtrack of a young child's life. Emily says this – "No!" – at school when her teachers ask her to stay in her seat during lunchtime, on the sidewalk when her mother tells her to get in the stroller, and at home when her father instructs her on how to connect the toy train tracks. She says this repeatedly as she and I play Duplos on the floor in her living room during our interviews; I assume the role of teacher as we build her classroom out of plastic bricks, my Duplo-figure asking hers to clean up. There it is, the same bold phrase, this time ventriloquized from Emily through her Duplo-figure, just as adamantly stated as she does in real life: "No! I don't want to!"

Surrounded by teachers and parents trying to control her life, Emily's presence and self-expression takes the form of resistance – she is always saying "no" to adults as she pursues her own agenda.

Why are the daily lives of young children saturated with adult control? What happens to the child's agency in the face of this control? How did it come to be this way?

I've developed a concept through my research in which I term the over-extension of adult control into a young child's life *adult imperialism*. I use this term neither loosely nor meta-phorically but rather to meaningfully describe the relationship between adults and children I have observed and how I understand the historical context in which this occurs. *Imperialism* is of course a loaded term. It is important to see where I pull this from in order to properly locate it's specific and intended use, describing the nature of the relationship between two entities – in this case, between adults and children. A cross-disciplinary collaboration between social historians and developmental psychologists (Cahan et al., 1994) provides the inspiration and framework for how I use this phrase. The authors explore the interaction between social context and child development in America over the past 150 years. They offer a useful lens to explore this interaction as they describe the "imperial" practices of adults and the "native" practices of children:

> The imperialism here is of the adult world on the child's, the flood of discourse and objects that adults aim at children in an attempt to socialize them into the world.

Children have their own "native" practices, as well as those imposed by the adults, for while adults are striving to socialize the child into their world, other children are striving just as hard to socialize the child into the peer group's alternative culture. pp. 200–201

Adult imperialism describes the relationship in which adults over-extend control into a child's life, seeking to replace the child's native practices with more adult-like versions and leaving the child with an *imperial childhood*. This over-extension of control is not a biological necessity but rather a cultural construction. Individual development is not the sole factor to consider when understanding children; they are also products of a time and place – of history and of cultural practices. This book is about this time, and this place: twenty-first century middle- and upper-class American childhood, in which adult imperialism has taken hold. We have created a management system for young children that extends far beyond the typical mandates that adults fall back on when questioned about the subject, such as safety, biological dependency, and academic preparation. What if we changed this? What if we saw young children as humans who (also) matter, instead of (only) as undeveloped and immature, in need of repetitive instruction and constant supervision?

I share here my novel perspective on these questions and what adults can do to alter this imperial relationship with young children. I use a critical lens to deconstruct dominant practices and perspectives within the current field of early childhood and ultimately offer a different vision of what is possible in adult relationships with young children. Whereas books about parenting or teaching might offer strategies to convince the stubborn child to yield and offer compliance instead, this is not that book. This is about not-teaching and not-parenting, in the sense that teaching and parenting are focused on raising up, changing, or transforming the child into something they were not before the action the acts of teaching or parenting occur – into someone more mature, or more knowledgeable, or more skillful.

This is my message: The degree of adult control present in our children's lives diminishes their agency and thwarts their capacity to engage with the world in meaningful ways. Whole Neverlands are lost, extinguished. Children are cut off from the world and rendered useless. Parents and teachers can shift their relationship with young children by receding out of parts of their lives and granting them a broader, less limited exposure to the world. Children will still grow up: they will still learn cultural practices and ways of being, they will still shed their childhood and become adults. But before they do so, there is a rich culture of childhood that they express, a powerful presence they have *as children.* Adults ought to be imposing their will on young children less, giving them more time and space for their own ideas to flourish and take root instead of always insisting on compliance with their adult expectations.

Many would laugh this topic off as frivolous. Having spent the past 16 years in preschool classrooms, I do not. A critical examination of this relationship shows the damaging impact that omnipresent adult control has in the lives of young children.

There is another way. We can do better.

Preschool Teacher

I showed up at the JCC in Manhattan for my first day as a preschool teacher in September 2008. While we were preparing for the school year, my head teacher asked me, "So, why are you a teacher?" I responded with the eagerness of a freshman: this was my way of making the world a better place; some people march, some people run for office, and I chose to teach. I have always approached the classroom as a place of hope, brightness, and advocacy. I believe school can be used as a tool by children and adults to together make the world a more righteous and just place. School need not only be a place of learning and growth; it can be a place of social advocacy and societal transformation, even for our youngest students and citizens. I have never let go of a committed stance toward the classroom as a place of hope and advocacy.

I fell in love the moment I started teaching and I've never looked back. The three-year-old classroom was a confusing, busy place, full of life and movement, dripping with creativity, humor, and play. Our class photo from that year still hangs behind my desk: there's the child who ate playdough off the floor; there's the one who sneezed so hard she fell over; there's the two who are still best friends 15 years later; there's the squirmiest child in the group on my lap, his legs tucked between mine, my arms wrapped around his torso so he couldn't leave. This image of me physically restricting a child's body so he would meet the expectations of the moment is forever linked with my first memories as a teacher. Why do we insist on control? I wasn't uncomfortable with it then. I am now. And then there's Shannon, my head teacher that year. Shannon taught me how to teach. She was a graduate student at Fordham University just down the street from our preschool, and she would bring in ideas each week from her evening classes. She was committed, professional, and responsive to children – all things I strove to become. I watched her that year and did my best to keep up.

I joined the preschool just as it was adopting a Reggio-inspired approach to early childhood education, modeled after the schools in Reggio Emilia, Italy. The approach focuses on seeing the child as a citizen with rights (this was totally new for me) rather than only, primarily, a developing body with learning goals to accomplish before advancing to the next stage (which is exactly what I thought teaching was). These educational practices prioritize the concept that "children have the right to be recognized … as both source and constructors of their own experience, and thus active participants in the organization of their identities, abilities, and autonomy" (Malaguzzi, 1993). Reggio-inspired educators, I would learn in my first years of teaching, "co-author" and "co-construct" the classroom along with their students, building an "emergent curriculum" in which the curricular topics emerge from the child's play, passions, and questions. We spent countless workshops over several years learning about Reggio-inspired practices and folded them into our own teaching practices.

With teachers and students seen as fellow citizens of the same community, it is a teaching practice in which all voices matter, together. This necessarily centers relationships and dialogue over hierarchy and control, as described by Loris Malaguzzi, the inspirational founder of the approach:

> The interaction between children is a very fertile and a very rich relationship. If it is left to ferment without adult interference and without that excessive assistance that we sometimes give, then it's more advantageous to the child. We don't want to protect something that doesn't need to be protected.
>
> 1994, p. 4

> It's necessary that we believe that the child is very intelligent, that the child is strong and beautiful. Those who have the image of the child as fragile, incomplete, weak, made of glass gain something from this belief only for themselves. We don't need that as an image of children. Instead of always giving children protection, we need to give them the recognition of their rights and of their strengths. p. 5

I watched Shannon work with – *with*, as in, *in relationship with* – two students as they (together) slowly transformed a large cardboard box into a firetruck. They cut, taped, glued, and painted, with lots of mess and giggles along the way. The goal was, as Shannon explained to me, for the children to have ownership over the direction of the play while being supported by the teacher; for their ideas, not the teacher's, to drive the project. Shannon had observed the children playing "firetruck" in the dress-up area and so offered them a way to extend and deepen their play by creating their own firetruck – she was working with them to bring their Neverland to life. This was intriguing to me and became a driving motivator for my work to come, exploring how children's ideas can become manifest in the environment around them and the adult role in supporting (or alternately, if not careful, disrupting) this process.

Graduate Student

I set out to learn more and establish my teaching bona fides. Naturally, I followed in Shannon's footsteps and in 2010 enrolled in Fordham University to earn my master's degree in early childhood education in the evenings while teaching during the day. Many of the teaching methods I learned at Fordham I still use today to support children in their literacy development, skill acquisition, and conceptual understandings – they are productive teaching strategies that help children learn. Our textbooks taught teaching methods utilizing a "developmentally appropriate practice" whose "ultimate goal is to promote the development and enhance the learning" for students (Bredekamp, 2011, p. 71). These books taught us that "children do not intuitively know how to behave in all the ways" that are appropriate for a classroom and, therefore, "adults must teach children what is expected and how to conduct themselves appropriately.... The idea of 'teaching' children how to behave ... is the hallmark of child guidance in developmentally appropriate classrooms" (Kostelnik et al., 2011, p. 161).

Yes, I thought, all these things are true: children do not intuitively understand how to behave in a classroom; children are developing beings; learning does take place in classrooms. It's not that I disagreed with the basic sentiment, but I took issue with this as the lead motivator and orientation for the classroom teacher. This is not a Fordham thing but rather a preschool teacher thing – the texts and practices I learned at Fordham are widespread and used broadly throughout the field and in every preschool classroom I've ever stepped foot in. Teaching children how to behave and to "conduct themselves appropriately" did not line up with my view of the role of the teacher. Shannon, and a Reggio-inspired classroom, had shown me that a different lens altogether was possible – for children's thoughts to change the classroom (in contrast to the classroom changing the child), for the curriculum to reflect the child's passions rather than prepare them for the next stage, for teachers to listen to and partner with children instead of telling them what to do.

One memorable course at Fordham was about a play-based preschool curriculum. The class was good, the theories were strong and helpful; I loved the class, and I became a better teacher. And yet, I slowly became troubled (sheepishly so, at first) at how we were asked to use play as a vehicle for teaching children math, literacy, and socialization (only) rather than (also) *learning from the children* about who they were, how they saw the world, and what they might create when given the time and space. The textbook for the course, *Play at the Center of the Curriculum* (Van Hoorn et al., 2011) was not interested in any of that: "Early childhood is an important time in the lives of our future citizens. The stakes are enormous" (p. vii). Play was to be placed "at the core of developmentally appropriate practice" (p. xiii), utilizing what we know about child development to operationalize play as an instructional method. Hold on, I thought. Were Shannon and the students playing firetruck because of the "stakes"? Because these three-year-olds were "future citizens" who needed to learn "how to behave"? This did not adequately describe my classroom or the interactions between children and adults I was seeing. It was missing something. Play was important to my students *because it mattered to them*, not because of the stakes, not because of where it would lead them in life. It seemed almost corrupt – to take something of such import to those who directly experienced it and operationalize it for future gains.

Back and forth I went, from Fordham at night to preschool each day. In my second year in the classroom (this class photo, too, is still on my desk), Zoe, three years old, would arrive at 8:30am each morning with her best friend Avery and settle in at the wall-mounted painting easel. They would transform into painters – not people who were learning *how to be* a painter (this is my play textbook's "future citizen"), but people who were meaningfully painting, *now* (this is Malaguzzi's "intelligent … strong … beautiful" child). Parents and teachers are so often blindly focused on the future pathways for our children that we fail to realize that for the children, *this is not preparation* – this is really happening and this is really authentic.

What she needed from us teachers was essentially to curate the environment. We would make sure the easel was ready for her each morning: red, yellow, and blue paint bottles, fresh paint cups, and a bunch of clean brushes. We would help her retrieve her painting from the drying rack and clip it onto the easel. Once armed with those materials, all she needed from us was patience and space. Zoe would patiently squeeze paint out from the large bottles into the small cups at the easel, select her brushes carefully, and proceed with slow, intentional, brushstrokes. She would paint daily until we told her it was time to stop for our classroom's morning meeting (9:00am – morning meeting was always 9:00am); we would help her carefully move her wet painting to the drying rack for her to pick up again the next day. She did this for months until she deemed her painting complete – a butterfly – and took it home.

Five years later, I could barely believe it when I ran into Zoe on the city bus, and she was sitting with the same best friend from the easel. After excited "hellos," I let them know that alumni are also welcome to come back and visit. Zoe was quick to say, "I would teach art to them!" Avery looked at her longtime friend and said with a twinkle in her eye, "Remember, we would come in early each morning and do painting?" Zoe looked at me and my heart melted: "Yea, remember the butterfly painting I made? I still have it. It's framed in my apartment!" When I arrived home that evening, her mother had emailed me a picture to prove it – there was nine-year-old Zoe, beaming in front of her master-piece, framed on her bedroom wall. I have always held on to this lesson – children's creative outbursts are not a collection of whimsical non-sequiturs. They matter deeply to the intelligent, strong, beautiful child who dreams them up and those dreams live on in the child long after the act of creation is done. Neverlands don't just disappear, but the context in which children are allowed to explore them does. Zoe and Avery came back to visit preschool as alumni later that year and they left a note on my desk before leaving: "It feels nice to be back! Can I re-wind my whole life? Please? The State tests are coming up!!!" They were in fourth grade. Over the years, school and the accompanying high doses of adult control train the Neverland out of our children.

I've pondered a long list of related questions ever since then: Why did we tell Zoe to leave her artwork and come to morning meeting? Was our meeting and its routines more important than her butterfly? Why didn't we just let her keep painting? Why did teaching mean telling children what to do? Why was the class-room built around ordering children's activities? There is an easy, developmentally appropriate answer – because Zoe had to learn how to behave in a classroom, which meant timely transitions into group activities, so that she would be ready for the state tests in grade school. Just like the squirmy three-year-old in my lap, I wasn't uncomfortable with it then. I am now.

In the preschool classroom, sharp bursts of freedom and creativity for the children during free time are demarcated by moments of control as students are moved through their time-bound daily schedule: now it is time to sit, now it is time to sing, now it is time to eat, now it is time to run. It all seems oddly tautological – children need to learn how to behave in a class-room setting, because they spend time in a classroom setting. Free play is restricted to certain parts of the day, which are scheduled, of course, and not naturally occurring – as if to say, "now it is time to be playfully creative." Free play is when what children say and do actually matter, when students can act on their own volition to determine their own activity, taking their ideas and bringing them to bear within their world. These are the moments in which to see children's generative power – when we adults move aside a bit and leave them lots of empty space. In my classroom, the children's Neverlands came tumbling out with force as they created fantasy scenarios in their play: they flew on the backs of dragons, escaped from pirates, took care of babies, preformed rock and roll shows, raved at dance parties, and painted masterpieces. These acts of creation were joyful expressions of who the children were and what the world meant to them. There was the time my students created a hot dog stand in the block corner that lasted for months (in a truly New York City moment, the children used playdough to plug the cracks between the blocks, Jake and Zak told me, "to keep out the rats"), and the time Ruby taped a piece of yarn to a marble and showed me her new "yo-yo" as she yanked it up and down. I can still see her proud smile, dimples in both cheeks, as she showcased her creation – she had brought this to life with her own ideas and ingenuity. This mattered to her, profoundly: *it* was here because *she* was here.

And then she had to put it down and go to snack time. We interrupted her Neverland not because she was hungry or done with her yo-yo, but because the schedule said it was snack time. In the preschool classroom, compliance overpowers generativity.

The problem is, I've never met a young child who runs out of ideas. When given time and space, children are ceaselessly generative, constantly dreaming up and exploring new possibilities as they navigate the world. This is the power that children have. We adults do a great job of diminishing this power as we attempt to regulate their lives. Despite the freedom during play time, adult control dictates the bulk of the preschool day as activities necessarily follow their predetermined times. The hot dog stand must be shut down and the marble yo-yo cast aside so that the class, as a whole, can go to the playground, or music time, or lunch, because that is what the schedule calls for. "Teaching" means inserting adult expectations into children's activities, behaviors, and schedules. This is not always necessary, welcome, or productive.

I knew my students had agency in a way that was not fully recognized (and often downright thwarted) by the institution in which they spent their days. By now I had graduated from Fordham with my Masters and was ready for the next challenge. I was presented with an opportunity to dive deeper into these ideas in 2013 as our preschool director, Ilana Ruskay-Kidd, left the school. Ilana had watched over the years as some of our preschool alumni were counseled out of their independent elementary schools due to their learning differences. This did not sit well with her and so she responded to the problem by founding a new school catered specifically to their needs. The Shefa School would become the first Jewish day school for children with language-based learning differences (*shefa* is Hebrew for abundance – as in, these children had an abundance of strengths, they did not need to be seen as deficient). Ilana showed me the possibilities of schools: they did not need to (only or primarily) shape children's behavior but in fact could (also) be shaped by what children needed. School need not be defined by attempts to conform children to its expectations.

If the child is unable to meet the school's expectations, perhaps it is the school that needs to change, not the students. This left a lasting impression on me, a shift in orientation. Like Shannon, Ilana was a strong model for me; as a preschool director now, I still often find myself contemplating, "What would Ilana do in this scenario?" Ilana was a model of grace and kindness, of prioritizing values and relationships over teaching strategies and learning milestones. Children were people first, learners second.

This lesson would also stick with me.

Preschool Director

After five years teaching, I applied for Ilana's now-vacant job. I left the classroom and became the school director. I was able to zoom out to explore the tension between adult control and child agency with a broader group of teachers, parents, and children. I took the lens that I had been developing in the classroom and could now apply it on a larger scale. As I looked at the school, in this new role, I saw the same pattern everywhere: as teachers and parents encountered child behavior that surprised or confused them, or was divergent from their expectations, they sought out strategies to shift the child's behavior back within expectation. These strategies sought to control the child by coercing them into desired behavior, such as sitting at mealtime or listening during story time. I felt sort of like a spy behind enemy lines, imploring teachers and parents to shed these strategies of control and to instead earnestly listen and dialogue with their young children. Maybe it was our relationship with children that needed to change, not the child's behavior.

Perhaps we can listen to children and get to know them, instead of commanding them to be more like us. Our tendency as adults is to assume that our expectations are correct and that if we simply find the right strategy, we can shift the child's behavior to meet our social standards. This is, after all, what contemporary parenting and teaching seem to be all about: aggressively convincing children to be more like us, the adults in their life – social, mature, regulated – and less like themselves – eager, frenetic, and idiosyncratic. This is a tendency that we bring to bear in nearly all of our interactions with children. We all – adults and children – might benefit from critically reflecting on this stance.

I developed a set of critical ideas and questions around these strategies of control and fleshed them out with parents and teachers. I began inserting these ideas into my weekly "Noah's Notes" (following Ilana's practice, I wrote weekly to our preschool families about preschool, children, and community, a practice I still maintain) and would explore them further with parents in recurring Coffee Chats in my office (first monthly, eventually weekly, a dozen or so parents chatting over coffee in my office after dropping their child off in class). Maybe, just maybe, there were ways in which we could chip away at the regimented control that adults hold over children's lives, giving them more space to be themselves, to find their own way, to express their own ideas. I was nervous to be bold – most preschool parents, in my experience, want more control over their children, not less, and so I was going out on a limb.

I explored this in one of my Noah's Notes:

September 2018: What does it look like to move away from strategies of control and towards relationships of trust?

For better or worse, contemporary society doesn't prepare us to trust our children. It prepares us to measure them, to teach them, to train them, to schedule them. So, when we pivot into looking at "relationships of trust", though it seems simple enough, it can often feel like stumbling in the dark. We're out of practice.

Andrew Solomon, in his epic "Far From The Tree", writes that parturition is not the act of re-producing, despite the common parlance. It is an act of *production*. Trusting your child means that you have accepted that you have created them, you have not re-created yourselves. It means that you accept both who they are *now* and who they are on the road to *becoming*. When we accept that, we are no longer compelled to control (as many) parts of their life.

I reviewed a few ways that parents can do this, such as:

Don't meddle in the details. Set up some routines (we clean the living room before dinner, we get dressed before we leave the apartment, etc.) and then don't worry about the small stuff in between. So their idea of "playing trains" is throwing tracks back into the bucket? OK. Their idea of "arts and crafts" is smushing together dozens of pipe cleaners in no discernible manner? OK. Their idea of a playmate is running around like lunatics with their shirts off screaming at the top of their lungs? OK.

Children do not live our lives. They do not have our outlook on what is right, proper, and appropriate. I promise you, they *will* learn all of that over time. But trying to control a three-year-old in the midst of an impassioned screech-fest only gets you a tense relationship and a breach of trust, it doesn't actually get you a gentler, more mild-mannered child. Showing a child what they "should" do with pipe cleaners just leaves them feeling less-then-capable and still-not-as-awesome-as-my-parent.

Just take a deep breath, accept it, note that kids are supposed be kind of wild and crazy, and focus on something else.

The next day, I got a supportive email back from Becky Kennedy, a parent of two in our preschool (who would soon become Dr. Becky): "Just wanted to let you know that your note detailing ways to do more 'trust' and less 'control' is amazing. Really really fantastic. Will reference it for a while!" Buoyed by positive parent feedback and enthusiastic engagement with the topic, I kept going.

During my second year as director, I began my doctoral studies in curriculum and teaching at Teachers College, Columbia University with a focus in early childhood education.

My head swirled as I dove into the world of critical progressive theories like neo-Marxism, critical race theory, postcolonialism, poststructuralism, and on and on. I was back in school at night and preschool during the day, loving it again. Two things happened at this point.

First, I realized that there was so much more out there in terms of educational theory than I had been exposed to during my Master's degree and my time as a classroom teacher. Simply put, it didn't have to be this way – there were other ways of seeing the world, of understanding relationships, of describing knowledge. I remember having a visceral reaction to texts like *Deconstructing Developmental Psychology* (Burman, 1994) and *Deconstructing Early Childhood* (Cannella, 1997), books which tore apart the foundations of the field of early childhood education and reframed everything I thought I knew – despite my already critical stance, they pushed me further afield than I had wandered on my own. Preschool classrooms, from this radical perspective, were understood as a tool used for children "to be isolated from the rest of the world and regulated through a controlled exposure" (Cannella, p. 30). Their far-out stance was hard for me to swallow – I remember putting the book down and not coming back to it for months (as a preschool teacher, to be honest, I felt disgusted at first) – but it pushed me in the right direction, eventually showing me a path toward answering my questions around control and agency. I did eventually pick it up again and now use the ideas frequently in my work. It can take a while for new ideas – for radical ideas – to settle.

If I am as bold as I'd like to be with this book, perhaps you may have the same reaction. This can be jarring and difficult to reconcile with your practice as a teacher or parent. It is not an easy thing to re-orient one's practices. But stick with me. Stay critical but try to keep an open mind.

Second, I was so glad that I had chosen to undertake my doctoral studies while still engaged in a job that kept me on the ground every day in preschool. This kept me centered throughout my studies, always forcing me to find the praxis, the pragmatic implications of the theories I was developing. Evenings spent in class, devouring texts and engaged in academic debate, were balanced out by days spent playing blocks and playdough in classrooms or in my office with parents. Tamar Schapiro's words rang in my head ("We do not feel bound by children's expressions of their wills in the same way that we feel bound by adults' expression of theirs") as I watched parents drop off their children so that teachers could organize their next few hours, until they were released to caregivers or parents in the afternoon, who would then organize the child's remaining hours until bedtime, all with an emphasis on compliance and obedience.

Preschool is a fun place. Definitely. But it's not quite Edenic – there are a lot of really hard moments for a lot of children, around separation, transitions, socializing, and the general cognitive and emotional load of "holding it together" all day long. All those tantrums they throw at preschool pickup are because of how much work it takes to successfully navigate a preschool day – it is their reaction to the system we have created for them. I kept thinking: but the kids never signed up for this! The "expressions of their wills," to use Schapiro's phrase, is completely bypassed in early childhood education in favor of maintaining the organization and schedule that society requires, regardless of how the actual human who goes through the experience thinks or feels about it. Preschool is conscription.

The ping-pong of theory by night and practice by day kept me grounded. *There, there,* and *there* – I could point out specific moments in the school day that brought theory to life.

One of them occurred every day in a very innocuous fashion. Each morning as director, I would stand in the main entryway to the school to greet children and their adults. Mostly, adults returned the greeting verbally along with eye contact and maybe a wave or a hug (preschool is a friendly place!). Students were of course broader in their range of responses – from a mile-wide smile and an enthusiastic high-five to hiding behind their adult's legs, eyes cast down, chin tucked into shoulder, burrowed deep away from social contact. Adults were frequently dismayed or unsure in those moments, a trend I see through to today as I continue to greet children entering school. A typical adult response to a child's hesitancy in the morning greeting is to implore their child to, "Say 'good morning' to Mr. Noah!", often followed by a mocking groan by the parent or knowing roll of the eyes. For some, this would escalate and become a pitched battle, with the adult-child dyad stuck in the doorway until the child complied. I wrote about this in a Noah's Note:

> *December 2017*: It is one of my absolute favorite parts of my job – helping children start their day at school with a smile and a friendly face. And every day, at least several children are hesitant to say "Hi" or "Good morning" in return. To respect the child's agency, I am interested in shifting our culture to one in which those children are not compelled to respond in an adult fashion, but rather are able to watch their adults provide model behavior. I am asking you to greet me how you want your child to, rather than mandate that they perform accordingly on the spot. I am fearful that if they are required to respond in a particular fashion, the intention of the greeting (warmth, safety, friendliness) is diminished in the face of adult imperialism – extending our control into their lives.

It was plain for me to notice that if an adult didn't respond verbally or make eye contact, it was not my place to call them out on it. It would be socially absurd for me to pause a parent to remind them of proper greeting protocol, but as Schapiro points out, we don't think twice about correcting and controlling a child's actions. I was no longer OK with how comfortable we are with telling children what to do, prescribing the specifics of their actions.

Ethnographer

At this point, I undertook three pilot studies through my doctoral coursework: the first for a week, the second for a month, and the third for three months, all aimed at the same core questions – why adults control children and what happens when they resist. In each study, I used ethnographic methods to explore the daily life of a young child. Ethnography is a qualitative methodology in which the researcher enters the subject's social environment to collect data through observations and interviews. This allowed me to escape the confines of the particular setting (such as classroom or home) and embrace the fullness of the child as they went through the various locations and institutions of their life. The pilot studies gave me the chance to hone my methods and grow comfortable with my role in the field before I embarked on a more complete study with Emily.

The ethnographic methods I use are called "participant observation," describing my non-invisible role: I was there (in the saloon window, remember?), with my research subjects, participating with them in the world while I also observed and recorded. This contrasts with other methods in which the researcher gathers data outside of the subject's naturally occurring social world by scheduling data collection, such as interviews, tests, and assessments, during specific times in specific locations such as offices, clinical settings, or special classrooms. My methods were largely inspired by, among others, the massive research project undertaken by Jonathan Tudge and published in the 2008 book, *The Everyday Lives of Young Children: Culture, Class, and Child Rearing in Diverse Societies.* His research has a focus on "the typically occurring engagement in everyday activities" between young children and "the people who spend a good deal of time with them" (p. 90). By using the child's actual social world as the field of study, the ethnographer attempts to observe human behavior as it occurs, where it occurs. This is why ethnography is a common method used for studying local or indigenous cultures – or in my case, the local, indigenous culture of childhood, nomenclature I began to use in describing childhood to highlight the intrusive role that I saw adults occupying:

Why are adults compelled to supplant children's indigenous culture by inserting their own imperial expectations?

I crafted methods that would allow me to develop a unique vantage point into those tense standoffs between children and adults and suddenly I found myself un-shackled by the perspective and responsibilities of a classroom teacher, a school director, or a parent – I didn't have to do anything "to" the child. In the role of researcher, I was not responsible for upholding the mandate of adult control but could begin to piece together the world from the child's perspective. I was no longer the one telling the children to clean up when play time ended, to slow down when they ran inside, or to stay in the stroller. This was a remarkable position to be in – an adult spending time with a child who they were not responsible for controlling. I found the uniqueness of the role, the novelty of the relationship, to be further motivation that I was barking up the right tree. I was enthralled with what seemed like an obvious and innocuous idea that was in fact quite radical given the contemporary paradigm of adult-child relationships – an adult can indeed spend time around children and not attempt to control them. There are other ways than control through which to know children.

The ethnographic methods used and developed during these pilot studies allowed me the unique vantage point of observing the child in all areas of their life. I adopted a "morning-'til-night" approach for data collection and visited the child in focus for three 4-hour observations conducted in consecutive weeks, stitched together to capture the child's typical social environment throughout the course of their day. I carried an audio recorder on a lanyard around my neck during all observations coupled with a trusty pen and notebook for capturing observations and stray thoughts into fieldnotes (these are called "jottings" in ethnography). The continually running recorder allowed me to capture the fullness of the child's life and I transcribed the audio files so that I could peruse the record of my time in the field. The life of a young child moves so quickly and fleetingly. I needed ethnographic methods to capture the fullness of these moments to later return to and analyze.

I sought out more literature on childhood agency to better understand the ways in which children push back against adult expectations, which led me to Dr. Anna Stetsenko, a psychology professor downtown at the City University of New York. I enrolled in her course titled "Agency and Social Transformation: Increasing Equity in Education," with each class session focusing on topics such as "Situating agency in context: struggles for social justice and democracy." She would change everything for me. Stetsenko was asking the exact questions I was asking but posed for a broader audience of educators, with a practiced boldness and intellectual acuity: Why did education tend to stifle the student's agency? Why did it seem that teaching was predicated on changing the learner? Was this the only way? The most desirable way? Stetsenko's work "invites researchers to become activists in the pursuit of new social arrangements and practices grounded in ideals of social justice and equality" (2009, p. 140). Yes! This was for me. "New social arrangements" was exactly what I was working toward, and now I could lean on the theoretical rigor Stetsenko provided to back it up. I would take her theories and apply them within the world of early childhood. I returned for two semesters of independent study with Dr. Stetsenko, embarking on my third pilot study under her direction and then ultimately crafting my dissertation research under her guidance – this was when I would meet Emily – along with my dissertation committee at Teachers College.

Stetsenko was singularly profound and intellectually explosive, which was exactly what I needed – she was extraordinarily well-read (putting it lightly) and never, ever, content with the status quo. Every time I left her office it felt as if the Earth had shifted under my feet. She was always striving, pushing to evolve both theory and practice. Over many conversations in her small office, with books and papers crammed on every inch of shelf space, she taught me that "social science is not canonical – it is about moving forward," that theory is used not only to better understand the world but also to shape it. For her, research is never neutral – researchers are part of the world and engaged in it, and therefore when in the field, she told me, "you are there with your commitments to overcome the present conditions." Research is about seeking justice, not only knowledge. She talked to me about social theories and "the grandeur of what the world-could-be, our sought-after-future, the distant horizon." "Without the horizon," she said, "we are enslaved to the current status." Yes again! It was indeed the distant horizon that I was after, a relationship between adults and children that seemed so far-off, so distant from the reality I faced in my own school and classrooms. Her point was well-taken and has animated my work ever since: strive toward that which is not yet present, not yet obvious, or understood. Do not be afraid of bold ideas or the work required to get there.

Stetsenko studied at Moscow State University in the 1970s and early 1980s, receiving her PhD in 1984, where she learned directly from Russian psychologist Lev Vygotsky's disciples and has since developed her own robust, radical extension of his theories and work. She has termed this the Transformative Activist Stance and it would become the underlying theoretical orientation of my work. Vygotsky is well-known to early childhood educators for his sociocultural theories of child development, originating the "zone of proximal development," highlighting the importance of play in a child's development, and illustrating how social interactions are key to learning. I knew Vygotsky from my coursework at Fordham and was familiar with how to apply his methods in a preschool classroom – how to use them to teach. But the Vygotsky presented to me by Stetsenko was something else entirely. Vygotsky was not to be treated as canon but as provocation; he was in every education textbook, but she was not settled with his ideas – they could be stretched further, expanded upon, used to generate still new ideas. Speaking in her office she said to me, "Vygotsky needs to be made dangerous again, that is, to be useful in the struggle for a better world." Hmm. This fit for me.

Vygotsky was dangerous in his own time, publishing then-revolutionary psychological theories in the 1920s that showcased the *social* and *cultural* nature of thinking, learning, and development – this is where the concept of "sociocultural development" comes from, a school of thought that would offer a new way to consider development as embedded within relationships and not only the individual child. His theories would posthumously be leaned on to create fields of study around the social nature of learning and development. This was in marked contrast to the prevailing behaviorist theories of his day, in which these processes were believed to take place *within* the individual person, isolated from the influence of cultural practices or social relationships. These behaviorist theories held that change, learning, and development were individual, not social, processes. Vygotsky's radical new theories were seen as troublesome to the ruling class and the prevailing status quo – they were dangerous. His work was banned in Russia for decades and would only begin to surface in the West in the 1960s before gaining global recognition in the 1980s. Vygotsky was purposefully and productively disruptive – but by the time I encountered his work at Fordham nearly a century after his time, his works were stripped of their revolutionary flair and squished within mainstream teaching techniques: improving children's literacy development, enhancing children's attention spans, and generally supporting the goals of the education establishment to produce docile, productive students.

So, how to make Vygotsky dangerous again?

Stetsenko's monumental 2017 book, *The Transformative Mind: Expanding Vygotsky's Approach to Development and Education* (try reading it cover to cover, I dare you), advocates for "a transition from a relational worldview premised on the socio-political ethos of adaptation towards a transformative worldview premised on the ethos of solidarity and equality." This is dangerous! Within her worldview, people band together to create the world they want and deserve – rather than adapt to the world presented to them by those in charge (read that sentence again and place it within the context of a preschool classroom). This is not abstract; this is about the real work of real humans to reshape the world they encounter – from an early age.

She writes, "the theme of people *adapting to* the world continues to permeate much theoretical work and needs to be consistently challenged" (2017, p. 177). For Stetsenko and the Transformative Activist Stance, "adapting" to the world positions the child, the student, the learner as passively soaking in the culture they experience, simply replicating the world they are given. In contrast, her "transformative" stance re-positions children, students, and learners as fellow humans who meaningfully influence the world they meet. Instead of looking at how schools change children through teaching methods, she argues that people are "agents of their own lives, agents whose nature is to purposefully *transform* their world" (2009, p. 138). The Transformative Activist Stance places a primacy on human agency enacted through social relationships. Children – as humans – do not passively adapt to the world as it is presented; they actively transform the world through their agentive acts.

I nodded along: the more Stetsenko talked, the more notes I took. As Emily meets the world, big, meaningful things happen – Emily is changed *but so is the world*. Stetsenko describes this meeting as an "en-*counter*," stressing that humans do not simply adapt but that they "counter" the world they meet through struggle and contest. Humanity is bestowed with culture and art (Zoe's painting), revolution and creativity (Ruby's yo-yo) – it is our nature to create, to yearn, to impact. When two things meet, *both are changed*. To convince ourselves otherwise – that it is only us who change children, never them impacting us or our world – is to deny the child their humanity.

I had my questions about control and agency, developed as a teacher and director. I had my research tools, shaped as ethnographic methods at Teachers College. And now I had my theory, leaning on the radical agency that Stetsenko saw in each human.

"Questions. Methods. Theory." I had what I needed to create something new, so I forged ahead, toward the horizon.

Introducing Emily

I'd never met anyone quite like Emily before. Or, rather, I had, many times over, it's just that I hadn't paid this close attention. I was always busy parenting, teaching, or directing – actively trying to direct traffic, to control behavior, to shape young minds. That was the orientation of my relationship with young children. I taught, they learned. With Emily I was finally able to watch, to listen, to observe, to think, to ponder. I could finally come to understand what it's like to be two years old in a world built for adults. It was a fascinating journey that forever changed me.

I first met Emily and her family – Kate (mom), John (dad), and Susan (sister); all names pseudonyms – in May of 2017. My dissertation research with her would begin that June and conclude nine months later. I visited Emily three times a month for morning-'til-night ethnographic field observations. I left my apartment in the early morning darkness for the first monthly visit, passing the grocery stores just as they were opening, to arrive at Emily's apartment as she was waking up. I accompanied Emily and Kate as they walked a mile to preschool; I watched as Kate said goodbye and I settled with Emily into her classroom. I stayed for morning meeting, free play, and snack time. My second monthly visit would pick back up in school at snack time and last until Kate picked Emily up at the end of the school; the third visit each month would begin at preschool pickup and extend until Emily was put to bed. Sunup 'til sundown, I was there as Emily moved throughout her world.

When all was said and done, I had amassed 27 observations of Emily and 11 interviews with her, along with 4 interviews with her teachers and 3 with her parents. I transcribed all the audio recordings (1,400 pages worth) along with 4 field notebooks filled with jottings. I recorded everything I could see and used interviews and artifacts to fill in more context: the layout of Emily's classroom and apartment, inventories at home and school of books, toys, furniture, and art supplies; lists of family calendars, daily schedules, and dates of major milestones; student reports from the teachers, handouts from Parent Orientation, and flyers from gymnastics. After Emily visited the art museum, I followed up with a phone call to the Program Director to learn more about what I saw; I was in touch with the product management department and compliance managers at different toy companies to learn how their toys wound up in Emily's life. I spent that year observing and investigating what was going on in her life. The following year I spent sifting through the transcript and developing analytic codes to identify patterns, themes, and areas of interest. The process of creating the codes by exploring the data helped me understand what I had witnessed and respond to my initial questions. The codes I developed – think of them like organizational tags for different parts of Emily's life – helped me make connections from my ethnographic data to existing literature and build new theories to describe it all.

But before any of that, I'm excited to introduce you to Emily.

Emily likes frozen pancakes and frozen mangoes, straight from the freezer. She likes watermelon and guacamole; she does not like tomato soup or chocolate. Her red nail polish that she had when we first met didn't disappear until several weeks into our time together, slowly fading and chipping. Her smile shows a dimple on her left cheek. She loves playing dress up, but she really doesn't like to wear shoes. She typically wore a small ponytail, perched just above her forehead to the right side. None of these parts of Emily are in isolation, removed from the conditions of childhood and its interaction with adulthood. Her ponytail is not just a ponytail but is part of the patterns of her life, the daily reality she contends with.

Kate told me the ponytail "keeps the hair out of her face" and that she often puts the hair tie in "before she gets out of her crib." But Emily preferred what she called "crazy hair." I watched one morning as they arrived at school: Emily hopped out of the stroller, yanked the elastic out of her hair, and called up to her mother, "I want crazy hair today!" as she swirled her head around like a fan at a rock concert. Kate, never ruffled, asked her, "Why'd you take it out? Your hair's gonna be in your face all day. Is it too tight? You don't wanna have your hair in your face." The thing is, that is actually *precisely what she did want* (again, Schapiro: "We do not feel bound by children's expressions of their wills in the same way that we feel bound by adults' expression of theirs"). This little vignette captures much of Emily's life: "crazy hair" is something she wants, it's part of her little culture, of expressing herself, while her adults – generally her parents and teachers – try to convince her to find the more mature version of that culture, of that part of herself.

Even in her ponytail, agency and imperialism were entangled.

Emily lived in an affluent neighborhood and her family was within the top 10% of household incomes in the city. Her childhood was marked by many of the trappings of "concerted cultivation," a concept developed by sociologist Annette Lareau in her groundbreaking 2003 book *Unequal Childhoods* (*read her book! And to balance out my focus on affluent childhoods, read Andrea Elliot's absolutely breathtaking and immensely powerful* Invisible Child). Lareau's theory describes how affluent middle- and upper-class families "cultivate" their children through careful social planning in which "organized activities, established and controlled by mothers and fathers, dominate the lives of middle-class children" (2011, p. 3). It is the thoroughness with which this adult control "dominates" the child's daily life that I am concerned with. Concerted cultivation was recognized as a foundational concept in understanding family dynamics in the United States by a generation of writers on parenting, families, and childhood.

Lareau's concepts also captured well the dynamics I experienced as a classroom teacher and preschool director, as well as in my own role as a parent. In this sense, Emily's world was familiar to me. This was *emic ethnography*, meaning I was studying a culture I was a part of, in contrast to *etic ethnography*, where the researcher embeds themselves in a culture foreign to them. This emic perspective allowed me fairly comfortable access into the workings of Emily's relationships and cultural spaces. I fit in. It also helped me generalize what I saw in her life back into the preschools and classrooms I have worked in. In this sense, the research period with Emily felt like a life lived in parallel – I would leave my own family and young children in the morning and travel just a few miles to spend time with Emily; after the observation I would go one more mile to my own preschool, spending the rest of the day with thoughts and observations lingering in my head, watching as the same tension around power and agency played out again (and again and again) in front of me.

During my time with Emily, she encountered milestones or transitions often associated with her age: her parents took the side wall off from her crib to turn it into a toddler-bed, she (mostly) stopped using her pacifier, and she began potty training. She was near 50th percentile in both height and weight. She was, in many ways, remarkably unremarkable; she was a regular kid. Emily was convivial, gregarious, and chatty, almost always seeking out social engagement. The end of year report, prepared by her preschool teachers for her parents, described that,

> Emily has penetrating bright blue eyes and a charismatic smile…. Her emotional terrain ranges from quiet, attentive and pensive to playful and boisterous. Emily often seeks out preferred classmates.

This same end of year report also highlighted the quality that I was there to witness – resistance in the face of adult expectations:

Emily will persist in getting her message across until she is satisfied that she has been heard. For example, on a very cold day, Emily insisted on wearing her Dorothy style shoes to the roof, against repeated instructions from the teachers and only relented when a compromise was made, where she could wear her boots but would carry shoes in her coat pocket.

"Against repeated instructions" defines much of what I observed that year. However, while she was indeed in a state of near-constant resistance, Emily displayed a general calmness, only rarely, to use the colloquialism, losing it. She used resistance as a tool, as a productive element of her personality. It was just how she got by in the world.

Mornings in Emily's apartment were marked by yawns, coffee, and eggs, along with time to play and go over upcoming events; evenings, the family sat around the dining room table and shared about their day. Family departures in the morning – Susan leaving for third grade, John leaving for work (he would arrive home around dinner most nights, sometimes later) – and arrivals in the evening almost always contained hugs, kisses, and warm greetings. Kate previously worked in early childhood herself; during my time with the family, she was a stay-at-home mom and organized her family's affairs. Emily's family apartment was decorated with bright yet soothing colors and positive sayings, such as a framed yellow poster near the entryway that read:

NOTE TO SELF:
BE KIND
BE KIND
BE KIND

Our summer months together were filled with leisure – slow breakfasts at home, lots of time at playgrounds, and long, quiet afternoons at home in the living room. Kate was the prime adult in her life, and I became the third wheel, tagging along on little excursions throughout the city.

In September, Emily crossed the Rubicon and started preschool. My research timeline was designed to capture this transition after spending the summer becoming familiar with Emily, and her with me, so that I would enter school with her as a known and trusted presence. No longer at home with mom during the day, Emily would now spend her time in a totally new environment, with new adults, and new children. As a researcher, freed of the constraints and responsibilities of the practitioner, I could watch as Emily challenged the sheriff, resisting the expectations of her teachers. I could observe those standoffs from up close, paying close attention to how and why they occurred. This was an almost cathartic release for me, after so long spent in a position of control in my interactions with children. What I found changed the way I understand early childhood and preschool and transformed the way I interact with children. At its core, Emily changed me – I did not change her.

What I learned from Emily would offer me a radically new vision of childhood, one in which "parenting" and "teaching" are shifted as we stop focusing on *what we want children to do and be* and instead focus on *who children are* and *what they are doing right now*.

References

Bredekamp, S. (2011). *Effective practices in early childhood education: Building a foundation*. Pearson.

Burman, E. (1994). *Deconstructing developmental psychology*. Routledge.

Cahan, E., Mechling, J., Sutton-Smith, B., & White, S. H. (1994). The elusive historical child: Ways of knowing the child of history and psychology. In G. Elder, J. Modell, & R. Parke (Eds.), *Children in time and place: Developmental and historical insights* (pp. 192–223). Cambridge University Press.

Cannella, G. S. (1997). *Deconstructing early childhood education: Social justice & revolution*. Peter Lang.

Elliot, A. (2021). *Invisible child: Poverty, survival, & hope in an American city.* Random House.

Kostelnik, M. J., Soderman, A. K., & Whiren, A. P. (2011). *Developmentally appropriate curriculum: Best practices in early childhood education.* Pearson.

Lareau, A. (2011). *Unequal childhoods: Class, race, and family life.* University of California Press.

Malaguzzi, L. (1993). *Una carta per tre diritti/A charter of rights.* From "The Hundred Languages of children" exhibit catalogue. Reggio Children.

Malaguzzi, L. (1994). *Your image of the child: Where teaching begins.* Exchange Press Store (3) March/April, 1994. Accessed online May 22, 2024. https://www.exchangepress.com//article/your-image-of-the-child-where-teaching-begins/5009652/?credit_success=1

Schapiro, T. (1999). What is a child?. *Ethics: The University of Chicago Press Journals, 109*(4), 715–738.

Stetsenko, A. (2017). *The transformative mind: Expanding Vygotsky's approach to development and teaching-learning.* Cambridge University Press.

Tudge, J. (2008). *Everyday lives of young children.* Cambridge University Press.

Van Hoorn, J., Nourot, P. M., Scales, B., & Alward, K. R. (2011). *Play at the center of the curriculum.* Pearson.

2

An Imperial Childhood

The Box of Being Two

Emily's world revolved around being two years old – whether she liked it or not, whether she wanted it or not, whether she knew it or not.

Her age was the single major factor that the adults in her life used to determine the parameters of her world: where she spent her time, who she spent her time with, and what she spent her time doing. Age-related expectations seemed essentially "inescapable," a word I kept jotting down in my fieldnotes as I crafted this concept. I began using the word "conscript" in my notes, referring to how the age-based requirements of childhood were imposed upon her by others. I began writing about a "conscripted childhood" from which Emily could not escape – adults shuttled her through life and paid more attention to her age than her volition. Childhood – the specific version of childhood offered through the concerted cultivation of middle- and upper-class families in America – was mandatory. As a conscript, where she went and what she could do was predetermined by her age and had nothing to do with how she might have made her own decisions if given the chance. Emily's participation in this version of her life was compulsory.

It was helpful for me to imagine this as a box in which she was trapped – at times it appeared Emily was banging on the walls of the two-year-old box surrounding her life, saying, "I don't

DOI: 10.4324/9781003455929-2

fit here! This does not define me!" This banging – the resistance against what adults expected of her – would be where I found her agency. And yet, her muted, muffled voice was discarded as the adults around her defaulted to the box – to the prescribed notion of what they thought two-year-olds should do and be. Conscripts can't just walk away.

Working in a preschool, I understand these age-related expectations well and use them every day. Across the country, at every preschool, age is the *lingua franca*. We use age first to sort and categorize children and then to create expectations for what they do and how they perform. In preschool, age goes from being a useful tool to becoming the omniscient answer to nearly every question: What classroom should this child go in? How many classmates will they have? What toys can they use? What activities can they participate in? All answered by age.

Until my time with Emily, I had never really looked at this system critically or wondered where it came from or why we used it. I had assumed, like most of us who work with young children, that this age-based ordering was both biologically cemented and historically eternal. That's how it is taught to us as preschool teachers: age matters, so learn it and operationalize it. Make use of it. That would change because of Emily as I began to uncover how the age-based groupings and expectations of children found in contemporary childhood are historically deviant and not necessarily the most productive lens through which to view the individual child.

Age always came first in Emily's relationships with adults. Adults insisted on calling attention to her age and using that as an enduring reference point for everything else about her. Everything I saw Emily do was placed within an age-graded context by the adults around her. We default to age, and our related expectations of who children are at that age, over the obvious capacity that children display in front of us. So much of the child's personality and contributions are lost as we smush them into the box of childhood. We see the two-year-old but miss the human.

On a cold December afternoon, just before holiday break (Emily's cubby was jammed full with a pink snow suit and jacket), I chatted with Tanya (one of Emily's teachers, we'll meet her shortly) while Emily and her classmates napped. Emily was tucked under her blanket, pacifier in her mouth, snoozing away. In a posture familiar to me, I tucked my legs into the Lilliputian furniture – us adults sitting on 10-inch chairs, our legs awkwardly tucked to the side or sticking out under the child-sized table in front of us. Describing Emily's play interactions with her peers, Tanya said that Emily's "language is very sophisticated for her age" and yet explained, "it's just, she is still a toddler, no matter how mature she acts – she is still a toddler." This is a culturally contrived stance that would pop up often during my time with Emily, as adults would observe Emily's various, textured interactions and yet boil her identity down to a single point of emphasis – age, and age-related nomenclature like "toddler." I noticed this pattern in which adults ignored the actual-human-being-Emily in front of them and instead replaced her with a normed-two-year-old. As Tanya and I chatted, her co-teacher reached between us to place a toy on the table we were at, to be available to the students when they woke up. It was a bucket of Bristle Blocks; I picked up the bucket to look for, and found, the inevitable sign: "Recommended for children2+." Well, these Bristle Blocks were certainly in the right place – they fit snugly inside the box of being two. Emily was "still a toddler" and so these blocks were for her.

Like Tanya (this kept happening), Kate also described how Emily's verbal strengths were mismatched with the age-based expectations placed upon her. Kate compared this to when a child is physically larger than one would assume for their age:

It's tricky too, because you know bigger kids always, you know, have these expectations when they are bigger for their age group. Like, my niece, she was a big kid, and she was wearing 5T (a clothing size designed for five-year-olds) when she was, like, three. So, everybody thought she was bigger than she was, and everybody put these expectations on her. So, I feel like I do the same thing, because I feel like I can communicate with Emily. (Kate pauses to laugh at herself) And I'm like "oh right – she's two." She would be in full meltdown, and then all of a sudden, she'll just stop, and say what she wants, and I'm like, "Wow!"

One idle June afternoon, Emily was in the playground sandbox as a new girl approached. As the girls built sandcastles together, the new girl's grandfather saddled up next to me and commented to Emily: "Hi little lady with the beautiful hair and the beautiful dress - just so beautiful! Oh my god! You are the cutest little thing - are you going to camp this summer?" Emily was bold and assertive, as always: "I'm not going to camp, I'm going to farm-out." (She was referring to "farm night out," an evening at Susan's day camp that the family would later attend.) The grandparent, impressed, raised his eyebrows high and smiled back: "You are very chatty for just a two-year-old girl! You're going to farm outing? That is beautiful! What an informative answer!" The grandfather was kind and curious … and incredulous about Emily's expressive capacity. Emily was a "little lady" who was "just" two and "the cutest little thing" with "beautiful hair" and a "beautiful dress." The surprise at her actual response belied the assumption that she was *only* those "cute" "little" traits, and nothing else. Emily's response was graded against the expectations of her age and was not considered a meaningful conversational element.

This was the inescapable box of childhood that Emily was conscripted into – each part of her personhood was refracted through the lens of her age by the adults around her.

The Little Ones

If age was the lever on which adults placed categorical expectations on Emily's life, then preschool was its fulcrum, the central point upon which those expectations rested. Emily's preschool was called Rainbow House, located on the two upper floors of a multi-purpose building constructed a century ago. Emily's class was called Little Ones, and her classroom showed the gentle grooves and odd angles of decades of love and use. The classroom, like Emily's apartment, was filled with love and warmth. It was a classroom I would have enjoyed being a teacher in it was a good place to be a child.

Little Ones had 11 students, all of whom were two years old prior to the first day of school; none would turn three until March later that year. The children all lived within a 2-mile radius around the school. The annual tuition was more than double the national average and shows a glimpse into the relative wealth of Emily's classmates and neighborhood. In addition to English, Emily's classmates spoke Spanish, Russian, and Hebrew. Morning drop off was done mostly by working parents, while afternoon pickup was done largely by caregivers; Kate was typically the only mother present for pickup.

Emily's class followed a consistent daily schedule: entry and playtime from 8:30 to 10:30am, then snack and a short circle-time meeting for a half hour, rooftop playground from 11:00 to 11:30am, lunch until 12:00pm then nap until 1:50pm, followed by dismissal and pickup. Reviewing the schedule, one can see a tightening of Emily's world. All summer long, her days were more whimsical and filled with long stretches of freedom. Little Ones would be a major shift for her, with a string of predictable transitions. For the first time, she would become a student, a title that will likely live with her for nearly two decades to follow.

I sat down with Emily's three teachers for a group interview in September just after the school year had started. Long legs, short table, we sat around chatting in our familiar-yet-awkward seating. Emily's teachers were gentle, kind, and caring. They were always thinking about how to engage their students with the materials in the room, responding to children's idiosyncrasies as best they could. They described that they worked to follow the child's interest rather than insert their own, which felt reminiscent of my Reggio-inspired training. Michelle, one of Emily's teachers, stated in our first interview that they strive to "cater to children's individual needs," and Tanya explained that "we try to put out something [in the classroom] that each child likes." Emily's three teachers each had their own path to the classroom. Michelle was born in the United States and came to Rainbow House right after her graduate work; she said the job "kind of just fell into my lap." Yasmin, born in Mexico, was a student at a community college prior to teaching and later transferred to a private university. Tanya, born in India, told me, "I come from a very different setting," and described vastly different approaches to many aspects of child-rearing from her own upbringing to her current work setting. Tanya moved to the United States at 26 with no experience in education. Settling near Rainbow House, she became familiar with the program after she started babysitting a student in the school and the director invited her to join as a teacher. Tanya was Emily's primary caregiver, a role designated by the teachers in which she would support Emily with basic tasks throughout the day, such as toileting and eating. Tanya and Yasmin both concurred that while Yasmin's relationship with Emily was "more of a friendship," Emily saw Tanya "more as the teacher" who had to be obeyed – or alternately disobeyed, as I would come to see!

In this first interview, I started from the top and asked the teachers how they begin each school year. Everything unfolded quickly and clearly:

Michelle: We get a list of all our kids, we get their addresses and where they live, and we start by reaching out to families.

Noah: How do the class lists get made?

Yasmin: It's by age group.

Michelle: You have to be two to be in this classroom, officially when you start.

I had the grandfather from the sandbox in mind ("just a two-year-old") and so pushed forward with age: "Why?"

Tanya: Because we are licensed from two.

Yasmin: That's because that's what we're licensed for, we're not licensed for anyone younger than that.

Noah:	And what about older children?
Yasmin:	You can't be three and start in this room.
Michelle:	A three-year-old would be in the classroom next door. So, it's Little Ones, there's Middle Ones I, there's Middle Ones II, and there's Big Ones. There's four classrooms.

"And what's the difference between the four classrooms?", I asked. The teachers spoke in chorus here. Michelle, "It's just by -," "– age -" Yasmin interjected, "– age -" Michelle concluded; "it's age," Yasmin reiterated. As we sat inside Emily's classroom, Michelle pointed first to the ground, "so the youngest are here," and then out the open door to the classroom down the hall to the Big Ones classroom: "and the oldest are there." Indeed, I looked down the hallway to see that each classroom door held a sign announcing the name of the room which doubled as a categorical description of its contents. It felt akin to the sign in a grocery store aisle, announcing cookies on one side and crackers on another, everything in its place: "WELCOME TO THE LITTLE ONES" read Emily's door; "WELCOME TO THE BIG ONES" read the opposing door.

The selection of the classroom name seemed so obvious – they are little, so call them Little – but I asked the teachers for their thoughts on "why the classrooms are called that." All three teachers seemed surprised at the question and raised their eyebrows in unison, as if it was either nearly heretical or stupidly obvious – we never question age or its implications because they are the bedrock of early childhood. Yasmin and Michelle responded, "I definitely don't know" and "I don't know the answer to that question." Tanya was more introspective, perhaps speaking to her longer experience in the school, piecing together what seemed like stray thoughts being assembled for the first time while speaking earnestly to the orthodoxy of the name: "Because, I mean, it's just a, it's just an identification – it's an identity – that this is Little Ones room – you belong to Little – *belonging* – of the child, when he's – when the child is entering, that he belongs to the Little Ones room."

Curious, I asked how this sense of identity and belonging was built, and Yasmin shared that they use the title of the class throughout the day to refer to the children, instilling in them that sense of belonging: "The first day of school, we say, 'Welcome to the Little Ones classroom' and we say, 'Little Ones, come to circle', we say when we go to the roof, like, 'Little Ones, we're lining up for the roof', so they hear it when we call them, line up, or we have circle, or the roof." This did indeed happen throughout the year, as I heard the teachers use the phrase repeatedly:

Little Ones, we have five more minutes left to play.
Little Ones, we have two more minutes until clean up.
OK Little Ones, it's time to clean up.
Little Ones, coming through!
We're walking back, Little Ones.

Young children like Emily are constantly being reminded about their age and stature. This is contemporary childhood epitomized: a dozen two-year-olds, lined up together, doing the same thing, going to the same place, following the same schedule, day after day, their "identity" and "belonging" oriented around a narrow window of dates of birth.

All these two-year-olds doing the same thing in the same place is so commonplace in today's childhood that we don't stop to question it. But this has never happened before, anywhere, until quite recently. It is *completely new* and *totally foreign*. We came up with this social arrangement only within the past century and yet it is so all-consuming that we have no idea how novel it is. Historian Paula Fass, a leading voice in telling the history of children and families in America, writes in her latest book, *The End of American Childhood: A History of Parenting from Life on the Frontier to the Managed Child* (2016), that adults who interact with young children are essentially blind to how we got here. She writes that many of the ways in which we think about young children today "float on anxieties that flourish without the understanding that would allow [adults] to make sense of how and why we treat our children as we do. We are self-conscious about childrearing without being truly aware of how our childrearing ideas developed (p. 270)." Parenting and teaching are not ahistorical – they are rooted in the past, shaped by those who came before, and informed by changing cultural conditions. To add depth to the theories I was crafting, I needed to know how we got here – the contemporary preschool classroom, related methods of parenting, and the broad formation of "early childhood" as a period of life.

How and why has age come to matter so much for how we group children? Why is the age span so narrow and specific? And what impact does this age-based segregation have on the lives of children? The various ages and milestones children move through are not necessarily as biologically linked as we assume. Crazy, right? An age-banded childhood turns out to be a socially constructed arrangement that reflects the cultural location of the child and not a singular biological or developmental truth.

Historical Childhood

For eons, the cultural distance between children and adults was quite small. Eating, sleeping, working, and socializing were typically communal activities, with little distinction between the location and activity of parents and children. Children were "immersed in the world of adults at an early age" (Heywood, 2001, p. 27) and "involved in almost all aspects of adult life" (Cole, 2005, p. 4) as they slept together with their parents, ate out of a communal pot at mealtime, tagged along and participated as work was done, and attended cultural events together. This had been true for, well, as long as humans had been around.

A *New York Times* article titled "Footprints Mark a Toddler's Perilous Prehistoric Journey" provides a glimpse into this. The article reviews anthropological research on footprints found in New Mexico that date back tens of thousands of years and show that "a toddler-aged child was being carried and periodically placed on the muddy ground as the caregiver readjusted his or her human load" (Kornei, 2020, online). The human footprints are intermingled among those of a giant sloth and a mammoth and indicate a pace that the lead author of the study described as if you were running to catch a bus. This toddler was definitely not in prehistoric preschool as her mom or caregiver ran away from potential danger. There was no stroller to put her in, no toys to distract her. Her identity was certainly not tied to being two, as Emily's was in Little Ones. She was right there with mom, alternately on her hip or hurrying to catch up. Historically, that's where children always were – right there.

Philippe Ariès essentially opened up the field of the history of childhood in 1962 with his seminal book *Centuries of Childhood: A Social History of Family Life* and reviews the long story of how it came to be that children went from being right there – on someone's hip or very close – to being sorted by age and isolated in a classroom away from family and society. Ariès makes the central claim that "in medieval society, the idea of childhood did not exist" (p. 128). This is not to say that children did not exist, of course, but that childhood as a notion, as a concept, did not exist in clear distinction from adults in terms of culture and society. If mom was on the run, so too was her toddler. While later historians have problematized Ariès' claim as overly broad and lacking nuance, I can certainly plug his statement into my research and claim with confidence – in the eras preceding my time with Emily, the idea of *her specific childhood* did not exist. Preschool, and separating young children from their parents, would have seemed like a preposterous idea. The key features of early childhood were nowhere to be found.

Beginning in pre-Enlightenment Europe, Ariès tells us that children of all ages were collectively referred to by a single word, the French *enfant*, and that the word had a "particularly extensive (1962, p. 25)" meaning. Extensive, indeed, when compared to the modern use of the word "infant," understood to refer to children who are no longer a newborn but not yet one year old. Proving this point, Heywood cites a ninth-century monk who refers to a 3-year-old and a 15-year-old both as "infants" (2001, p. 17), and Ariès finds material from 1556 which outlines the "first age of childhood" as the period in which "the teeth are planted":

...and this age begins when the child is born and lasts until seven, and in this age that which is born is called an infant, which is as good as saying not talking, because in this age it cannot talk well or form its words perfectly, for its teeth are not yet well arranged.

1962, p. 21

This "first age" spans the entirety of what we now call early childhood education, encompassing newborns, babies, infants, toddlers, preschoolers, and elementary school students along with the truly massive developmental transformations that occur during those years. Ariès also tells us that "baby" and "child" were used nearly interchangeably in English until the middle of the nineteenth century, with no specific word for the first months of life until the French turned the English "baby" into "bebé": "Henceforth, with the French word bebé, the very little child had a name (p. 29)."

I was intrigued – how baby became baby – and dove into my data; I remembered Emily had once asked the same question that Ariès just answered. On a snowy December afternoon, Kate helped Emily bundle up in the hallway outside of Little Ones for the walk home. Kate was describing to me Emily's sleep schedule and started from the beginning: "When she was a baby...." Emily overheard and sparked a curious discussion, showing off her familiarity with the modern nomenclature of childhood:

Emily: Mom, when did I become a baby?
Kate: What?
Emily: When did I become a baby?
Kate: When did you turn a baby?
Emily: Uh-huh.
Kate: Oh – well – you were a baby when you were born – and then maybe – I dunno – maybe when you were like one, we started calling you a toddler, remember?
Emily: But I'm not a toddler.
Kate: You're not? What are you now? Now you're a Little One.
Emily: Mm-hmm.
Kate: You're not even a toddler anymore!?

Emily: No!

Kate: Okay so you were a baby and then you are a toddler and now you're a Little One. What are you going to be next?

Emily: I dunno.

Kate offered an almost verbatim repetition later in the year: "You're not a baby, or a toddler really, you're a Little One," and another time, "You're not a baby, you're really a toddler." Emily herself moved fluidly between these designations as we explored the topic in our interviews on her living room rug, where we would set our Duplo-figures up in a pretend school. One time Emily offered up a humorous reflection as she bopped her figure through the play school: "I'm in Big Kids! I'm in Baby! I can be a baby. No – I'm a Little Kid! I'm not a bigger kid, cause I'm not in Big Kids." While she would play around with the different roles, she ultimately would always land on toddler, re-affirming to me several times throughout our Duplo interviews that "I'm a toddler."

The lack of cultural separation between children and adults would broadly hold steady in Europe throughout the Enlightenment in the seventeenth and eighteenth centuries and was then exported to colonial America. In early colonizing families, "parents and children worked together to produce everything they needed – including their food, clothes, tools, houses, and household furnishings (Cole, 2005, p. 4)." Little had changed over the centuries for childhood: activities that sustained the household continued to involve all of its occupants. Just like those prehistoric footprints, children were still right there, alongside their adults.

There was nowhere else for them to be.

Modern Childhood

The second half of the nineteenth century would inaugurate massive changes in the lives of children and their relationships with adults. The Industrial Revolution had recently begun to change the structure of work and family, as material goods became largely produced by machines instead of human hands. Work and family became separate for the first time as adults left their families – and the family economy that included children – for factories. More parents were absent from the home during the day and the household economy that had formerly included young children was essentially gutted by industrialization. Accordingly, school attendance for older children increased and gradually became mandatory. Along with other sociological and demographic factors, this "reframed the parent-child relationship" in ways that had profound consequences in the lives of children (Fass, 2016, p. 7).

Historian Howard Chudacoff describes how changing school attendance patterns impacted children's lives in the second half of the nineteenth century in his 2008 book, *Children at Play: An American History*:

> The increasing pervasiveness of graded public schools, with their enrollments swelled by compulsory attendance laws, herded kids together and fomented peer-group associations that kept same-age youngsters together for the better part of their waking hours. p. 86

By the end of the nineteenth century, children were sorted into narrow cohorts based on their age for large portions of their daily life *for the first time in 200,000 years of humanity*. After spending the entirety of our evolutionary history right there, alongside grownups, the importance and impact of this change on children and childhood cannot be overstated. Children were now largely separated from the daily lives of adults as they were pushed into a specific age range within their newly established "peer group." Compulsory schooling began to change the way that children interacted with society as "young people were being increasingly segregated from adults … notably in age-graded schools (Heywood, 2001, p. 29)."

Age began to matter in the ordering of children's lives. The steps were being laid for modern-day early childhood and Emily's eventual enrollment in Little Ones.

Emily understood well how this worked – how school was used to separate children into age-based cohorts. After we warmed up from the cold walk home on that snowy December day, Emily and I set up our Duplo interview scene in the living room. "This can be the teacher," Emily told me, as she waddled a Duplo-figure through the school and then spoke as the teacher to the students: "You need to be safe, ok? You just can't jump; you have to just be careful." The teacher's role in Emily's Duplo-school was always to say the rule. Susan, who had been snacking in the kitchen, came into the living room and sat down with us, picking up a Duplo-figure and starting to play. Emily was quick to tell her, "You can't come in!" Susan tried again – "Can I be a kid? Named Misty?" Emily thought for a second and quickly reconciled everything: "Um sure, but you can't come in school (she looked down at our preschool) – you have to go to your own school – to elementary school." I repeated the phrase back to her, as a question: "To elementary school?" "Mm-hmm," Emily confirmed as she nodded her head and pointed across the room, "That's elementary school, over that way." Susan left.

Older children are not the only people who don't belong in preschool – Emily understood well that parents are not allowed in either. In early November, Emily extended the Duplo-school scenario to include preparation at home and drop off – this was new for us, previously we had only explored things inside of preschool during our interviews. This time, however, Emily had Duplo-Emily get ready at home – taking a shower and getting dressed – and then walking to school with Duplo-mom. Arriving at preschool, Emily said, "I have to *bye-bye*, ok?" I couldn't make out which character she was speaking for (Emily or the mom) and so I asked, "Who is leaving?" Emily held up the Duplo-mom and said, "I have to, 'cause I'm the mom." It is obvious from the child's perspective: preschool is a place where young children are separated from older children as well as their parents. It is a place only for them and people like them, with teachers keeping order.

Compulsory schooling and age-banded classrooms were increasingly changing the lives of children as the nineteenth century came to a close. Little Ones, however, was still a far-off reality for a two-year-old. There was no dedicated cultural location or institutional space yet for a child that young: preschool and early childhood had not been invented. In this period, we can see the early seeds being planted that would eventually develop into a yawning gap between young children and adult society.

The first public kindergarten opened in 1887; 30 years later, roughly 10% of five-year-olds in the United States attended kindergarten; almost 150 years later, this number now hovers around 90% (National Center for Education Statistics [NCES, n.d.a]). Steven Mintz offers a compelling picture of the age group that would later become preschool and early childhood in his 2004 book, *Huck's Raft: A History of American Childhood* ("To any parent who isn't a professional historian, the book is a revelation," Jennifer Senior wrote [2015, p. 126]). Day nurseries, perhaps the ugly predecessor of today's preschools, were slowly starting to develop, with about 90 established throughout the nation's cities. They were not popular nor seen in the same light as today's preschools and daycares, serving a completely different function in society:

Most mothers kept their children in these institutions briefly, in part because the caregiver ratio was extremely poor. In one nursery, a single woman cared for as many as fifty children. Day nurseries quickly acquired an unsavory reputation... They were regarded as an unfortunate necessity for families in crisis rather than as an educational institution or as an institutional mechanism to allow mothers to work.

Mintz (2004, p. 179)

The day nursery was a place you went only when you had no other options. Today, about half of two- to five-year-olds attend some form of preschool care (NCES, n.d.b), and many preschools enjoy a prestige status and maintaining lengthy waitlists. The passion we have for preschool today would have been unfathomable to those mothers sending their children to day nurseries as a last resort.

Other features of early childhood today, such as playgrounds and toys, were in the same category as preschool at this point – just barely beginning to take their modern form. Joe Frost writes in *A History of Children's Play and Play Environments* that sandboxes built in Boston in 1886 are seen as the beginning of the modern playground movement (2009, p. 92). By 1905 there were barely 100 playgrounds in the entire country, and so children used streets, sidewalks, parks, and any open, public spaces as their play areas (Mintz, 2006). Playgrounds would become increasingly tame and risk-averse spaces in the century that followed as safety concerns replaced risky play (Cole, 2005). In her deliciously titled chapter, *The Politics of Dollhood in Nineteenth-Century America* (1993, Chapter 1), Formanek-Brunell writes that Macy's was the first store to offer a toy department in 1875 as the commercialization and mass-manufacturing of dolls was just beginning to take hold. Toys, if present at all in a two-year-old's life, were instead predominantly made by hand from scrap materials found at home. The wooden unit blocks kept on the shelves in Little Ones, now commonly found in preschool classrooms, would not be invented until 1913 by Caroline Pratt for her school in lower Manhattan. The Melissa & Doug toys designed specifically for two-year-olds, which we will see later in Emily's life, were completely absent in this era.

Things were changing for children in 1875, but Emily still would not have attended preschool or had playgrounds, manufactured toys, or a classroom. She would not have found a "belonging" or "identity," in Tanya's words, in being a Little One. Being two meant something different than it means today. Defining features of today's childhood were absent.

By the end of the nineteenth century, the dividing line between children and adults continued to grow, a trend that would continue right through to my time with Emily. At the turn of the century, middle- and upper-class families introduced something new to the household: a nursery room for young children. Formanek-Brunell describes how this development created, *for the first time,* a scenario in which "children lived apart from parents" (p. 19). Ariès uses the phrase "confined spaces" to describe how "family and school together removed the child from adult society" (p. 413). Barbara Rogoff, a cultural researcher who investigates variation between communities and the role of children, has written extensively about the impact of age-based segregation on children's lives. Rogoff writes from a sociocultural perspective, inspired by Vygotsky and his work to see children as "cultural participants, living in a particular community at a specific time in history" (2003, p. 10) rather than as isolated organisms unfolding in predetermined patterns. She describes how this modern separation of children from adults bars children from participating in "mature community activities" that they had previously been involved in (and still are, in many communities across the world), such as food preparation, caregiving, the production of goods, and cultural rites.

Rogoff's (2003) book, *The Cultural Nature of Human Development*, was a guiding force for me throughout my dissertation research and continues to occupy a regular space on my desk, it's cover marked by coffee stains and its pages dog-eared and marked up with my scribbles and reflections. Her cross-cultural work sheds light on how distinct this new social arrangement is – and on how Vygotsky's ideas can be used to animate the historical shift as children have been set apart from adult activities. She describes how school in Western society is "organized to keep children away from adult settings" (p. 140) and shows how the cultural arrangements in which children are raised are not biological destiny but rather manifestations of a particular time and place. And for Emily, that time and place meant that being two years old defined her existence. This is roundly agreed upon by critical scholars who find that "the structure of the school system" is designed to "exclude children from the world of adult work and confine them, instead, in the school room in the role of non-producers" (James & James, 2004, p. 7).

When children are in school with peers all day, their window to the rest of society is, at least partially and in many ways substantively, closed.

Controlled Childhood

Demographic changes would stretch the growing gap between children and adults even further throughout the twentieth century as families grew smaller, mothers joined the workforce, and women gave birth later. William Corsaro writes in his 2011 book, *The Sociology of Childhood*, that by the early decades of the twentieth century, these changes in family life led to "a resulting increase in the general institutionalization of children... [in] child care and early education institutions shortly after birth" (pp. 106–107). Here, finally, we see how today's age-banded preschool classroom emerges from a past in which "childhood did not exist." This was the box of being two that I was seeing in Emily's life – its historical roots lie in the separation of children from adult society that developed throughout the second half of the nineteenth century and continued to be cemented in the 150 years that followed.

Let's take a quick look at the numbers to see how this happened. The median number of siblings in an American family shrunk from an average of nearly seven in 1890 to under two by the twenty-first century (Corsaro, 2011, p. 106); by 2021, the average American woman gave birth to 1.66 children throughout her life (NCHS 2023, 2023). An only child is the fastest growing family type and seems on its way to becoming the norm. The presence of mothers in the workforce can be mapped alongside this trend: the percentage of children with working mothers grew roughly 10% during seven consecutive decades, from 10% in 1940 to over 70% in 2000 (Corsaro, 2011, p. 107). Linked to both of these trends is the delayed age of childbirth: in 1935, 70% of first births were from women under 25 years old (NCHS, 2011, n.d.); by 2008, 72% of college-educated women 25–29 years old had not yet had children (Brooks, 2018, p. 44). The average age of the American mother when she first gave birth in 1935 was 21 years old, in 1970 was 24.6 years old (NCHS, 2002, n.d.), and in 2021 was 27.3 (NCHS 2023, 2023).

The current norm of one or two young children in a family with parents in their 30s created a massive gap between the generations which had really never existed before. All of these trends are still moving in the same direction – fewer siblings, older parents, more working parents.

I'll pause here to make sure the numbers don't do the narrating. These historical trends are neither "good" nor "bad." Working, educated mothers and fathers who left the home for the factory a century prior did not "cause" this sociological reality. There are, no doubt, enormous benefits and privileges afforded to contemporary parents, *and children*, in the current arrangement, included among them the advancement of women, the protection of children from harsh labor conditions and sexual exploitation, and vastly improved life expectancies and health circumstances for young children. As Fass reminds us, it is important to know how we got here so we have a better grasp of where we are and what we are doing. Families are not static; they have always been changing. These are our families today.

Smaller families and older parents have had a massive impact on how parents interact with their children and the expectations they place on them. In essentially all previous generations of humanity, women gave birth from a young age and families comprised many children spread over many years with a wide range of sibling ages. The generational sprawl afforded children playmates, caretakers, and role models spanning a broad range of ages. This sprawl connected the generations, as the gap between them was less severe: children could participate in mature community activities such as being a caretaker for younger siblings and a contributor to the household economy.

No longer. As families shrunk, children became isolated from mature community activities and grouped away from children not in their specific age cohort. Rogoff again shows us how profoundly this departs from historical and traditional arrangements, many still found across the world. As a cross-cultural anthropologist, she describes how "in many communities" across the globe, "care of infants and toddlers is traditionally carried out by 5- to 10-year old children (2003, p. 122)." Her cross-cultural review includes examples such as in Polynesia, where she writes that "as they left infancy,"

...children became quite independent of parents and active in sibling and child groups. Once babies could walk, mothers released them into the care of 3- to 4-year-old siblings, who played nearby, checking periodically on the young ones. Mothers showed siblings how to feed and entertain 4-month-olds, handing them squalling babies to calm. Parents oversaw the children rather than being directly involved. Tasks were often assigned to the children as a unit, leaving them to decide who does what; all were held responsible for task completion. p. 123

The global arrangements of childhood that Rogoff describes highlight how social and cultural context matters for what we have come to call child development. Just like families are not static, childhood – and children – are not static. There is no everlasting, stable truth here. Who our children are, what they can do, and how they relate to the world is not a "pure" product of biological development. Our own cultural practices feed into the developmental possibilities ahead for our children. Emily's development reflected the cultural arrangements and developmental possibilities that concerted cultivation allowed for.

Overlapping with the demographic changes within the family over the past 150 years – indeed, made possibly *by* those changes – was the creation and robust growth of a "scientific childhood." Charles Darwin's 1877 article "A biographical sketch of an infant" is generally considered the first "scientific" account of childhood. We hear in a similar "biography of a baby" written in 1900 that "It is hard to get statistics about babies, scattered as they are, one by one, in different homes, not massed in schoolrooms" (Shinn, 1900, p. 10). Consider just how distant that is from today's world of early childhood: children did not yet exist in groups, they only existed in families. Accordingly, there was no "normal" for specific ages of children because, as a group, children had not been studied; there was no aggregated data. Children were not yet "supposed to" hit specific developmental milestones at hyper-specific ages (recall Ariès' "first age" lasting until seven). "Child development" could be summed up quickly: you had many children and as those that survived grew, their competencies grew, too; as they were ready, they took on more responsibility within mature community activities. This changed quickly as the number of scholars engaged in the study of children rose from just a few in 1918 to 600 in 1930, and wives' tales and folkways, transmitted mother-to-mother, were replaced by "the new experts – psychologists, pediatricians, psychiatrists (Fass, 2016, pp. 102–103)."

Science changed childhood. This is important for us to remember. This created a new type of childhood – a "normed" childhood, "in which the normal became the standard criterion for raising children" (Fass, 2016, p. 112). It was in that era that parents and teachers in America began to identify *specific* ages with *specific* milestones. Along came new expectations that *all* children at a certain age would be able to hit the associated milestones. Arnold Gesell would introduce his maturational theory of child development in 1925 after conducting what is believed to be the first extensive study of children's behavior, surveying thousands of children to determine patterns in development (this had literally never been done before). His theory introduced us to the idea that development was "fixed," which essentially meant that the child's life unfolds like a row of dominos – each step is supposed to occur in the right moment, in the right sequence. A century later, this idea has been nuanced, expanded upon, and problematized – children grow in all sorts of funky, idiosyncratic ways – but in practice this narrow, outdated notion of "fixed development" maintains wide sway over the field for teachers and parents. *"Every other kid is doing it, why isn't mine?"* became a common lamentation. Dr. Spock would pick this mantle up in the late 1940s and serve as the standard-bearer for the field of child development for the next two decades. Gesell and Spock, each in their own way, gave numerous gifts to parents, families, and children by elevating the importance of paying close attention to children and prioritizing their health and well-being. And critically, relevant for the questions I am asking, American parents and teachers were left with a legacy of seeing age-as-uniform as the primary lens through which we see, understand, and relate to children.

The early and enduring insistence on maturation and uniformity within the nascent field of child development betrays the era in which it arose and the now-discarded scientific disciplines that surrounded its origin. Consider the scientific environment in which the field arose: slavery, racism, and colonialism were all upheld by the purported science behind ideas like eugenics, a thinly veiled racism in which humans were to be sorted based on seemingly heritable qualities in order to purify humanity. "Science" was used to support the world order, and our understanding of children at the time was made to fit this episteme. Burman, one of the authors I had a hard time reading in my doctoral courses, writes how "the study of infants" in the late 1800s, just as the field was emerging,

> ...was related to similar ventures in anthropology and animal observation that were closely allied with European imperialism, maintain[ing] the hierarchy of racial superiority that justified colonial rule. The child of that time was equated with the "savage" or "undeveloped"; since both were seen as intellectually immature, "primitives" and children were studied to illuminate necessary stages for subsequent development.
>
> The apparently bizarre beliefs and behaviours of both "primitives" and children were seen as relevant to the understanding of neurotic and pathological behavior. A set of equivalences was elaborated whereby the conception of the child was related to the "savage", who, in turn, was seen as akin to the neurotic.
>
> These were the features that were taken up to structure the emergent developmental psychology. It should be noted that these views were widely held, and that, among others, both Freud and Piaget subscribed to them in their writings.
>
> 1994, pp. 10–11

Strands of child development originated out of ideas borrowed from those fields and thus wound up crafting development in fairly sinister ways. In the ethos of the era, you had to be a certain way in order to count. Science has moved on from this understanding of humanity, but its impact remains visible in the world of early childhood. Scholars critical of this lasting impact have described it's legacy as leaving children to be seen as "incomplete" until they reached their "full human status" by attaining certain developmental criterion (Dahlberg et al., 2007, p. 45). The scientifically normed child would come to dominate early childhood through the widespread adoption of developmentally appropriate practices – these are the textbooks and standards taught to aspiring teachers as they join the field of early childhood. Children of specific ages are supposed to do specific things and the teacher's job is to make sure that happens (or they might never become full humans!).

This normed childhood is not vague or ambiguous but quite specific and exacting. Since the 1980s, early childhood professionals have been expected to operationalize these new norms for young children through "developmentally appropriate practices," a concept which I find generally helpful – and overall, positive for children's quality of life, both at home and school – but deeply problematic in how it essentially flattens childhood, imposing (and I use that word very intentionally) the same standards on all children based solely on chronological age. A classroom teacher once described to me a preschool where she previously worked, where things were done "by the book – we gotta do *this*, and if they're not on *this* level, it's a problem." She meant "by the book" literally, as she explained that the curriculum and activities were pulled from a scripted curriculum book and the teachers were expected to "just print it and copy it and put it on the wall."

This is the "controlled exposure" that I had read about as a doctoral student in Cannella's book on deconstructing early childhood. I initially thought Cannella was being rhetorical or hyperbolic but have since realized the statement was meant literally. Demographic changes and a scientific childhood led to the creation and implementation of a new space for children which was limited, precise, and specific – early childhood education and developmentally appropriate practices. The teacher-training textbooks like the ones I encountered at Fordham spelled it out plainly, explaining the process of how developmentally appropriate practices are established and used in preschool classrooms: "we first think about what children are like within a general age range" such as "the number of [puzzle] pieces 4-year-olds typically find doable" (Kostelnik et al., 2011, p. 20). The same textbook provides a sample schedule for a "full-day program" within a preschool or daycare setting, suggesting a precise amount of minutes to each activity throughout the day, at a fairly rapid pace with many transitions: 10 minutes, 15, 30, 45, 10, 15, 10, 35, 10, 10, 10, 45, 15, 15, 45, 30, 45, 10, 15, 10 (p. 156). These standards came to be adopted by preschool classrooms and "age appropriate" became the guiding principle for toys, activities, and schedules. This pacing then spread from the classroom to every area of the child's life – museums, afterschool activities, nearly all cultural offerings. We've told young children they have short attention spans and then ensured it by always insisting that our assumptions are correct. The world that children interact with – the way the world is exposed to them – became tightly controlled by adults.

To get *many children* of the *same age* to do the *same thing* and accomplish the *same goals* at the *same time* is not easy, it turns out.

Imperial Childhood

Four books were published in my first few years as a preschool director that reviewed different aspects of why and how this happened and updated the history into the 2010s. These authors became my canon, my bedrock, as I ran a preschool while critically considering early childhood, developmentally appropriate practices, and why we forced children to comply. Published just as I was settling in as a director and finding my way at Teachers College, they were each deeply impactful in shaping my professional role and my emerging research: *All Joy and No Fun: The Paradox of Modern Parenting* (2014), by Jennifer Senior; *How to Raise an Adult: Break Free of the Overparenting Trap and Prepare Your Kid for Success* (2015), by Julie Lythcott-Haims; Fass' 2016 history introduced earlier; and *Small Animals: Parenting in the Age of Fear* (2018), by Kim Brooks. These were the authors having the conversation that I wanted to join – I wanted to extend the focus of their work down into the early childhood years. Each in different ways, they were talking about how societal changes impacted children's experiences at school and at home in ways that, essentially, held them back and shrunk their possibilities. Of this batch, Senior's book came out first. I attended a talk she gave in a neighborhood bookstore, and she opened my mind up to using a historical lens to consider the questions that I had been asking myself for a few years, about adult control in the preschool classrooms. It hasn't always been like this – it all came from somewhere. Reviewing these books together after spending my year with Emily, it all made sense – how we got here, to Emily's life, where everything she does is done under the controlling adult gaze.

Scientific breakthroughs for vaccines, medicine, and birth control miraculously allowed parents to have some say – some control – in their children's health and lifespan. By getting involved, parents could actually help their children live longer, healthier lives: "the ability to exercise some control in such life and death matters...introduced a major alteration in parenting possibilities" (Fass, 2016, pp. 218–225). Giving birth, at a specific point in life, became a choice for many women rather than an inevitability as women now had the "ability to change birth patterns... [through] medical devises and expertise...and more effective use of birth control" (Fass, 2016, p. 101). This "unprecedented expansion of choice...has changed the way parents approach matters of family life large and small" (Brooks, 2018, p. 48). Parents – their choices and their role in the child's life – began to matter in a very different way.

Besides the many obvious benefits of these choices, such as family planning and financial stability, this would prove pivotal. This "expansion of choice" that parents had when organizing their children's lives soon grew to include what type of preschool or care setting their child would attend, or if a parent would stay home to care for the child. Just like vaccines and birth control, these were new choices that families had not previously confronted. With the changing world – the creation of early childhood, the removal of the child from adult society, and the increasing choices that parents were able to make about the lives of their children – the role of the parent changed and now included the requirement to make endless decisions about the child's life. What type of crib to use, what type of monitor to install, what weekend activities to sign up for, what toys to offer, what type of birthday party to host, which playdates to set up, which stroller is best. All of these hyper-modern decisions that we have introduced are not actually parenting questions; they are cultural questions. They come from our needs, not the child's.

In a historically radical departure, the culturally mandatory role of the parent was now to sculpt the young child's life by making millions of informed decisions.

Along the way, a newly anxious zeitgeist was layered on top of the age-based expectations that came with this scientific childhood and paradigm of control. A "uniquely American product" (Fass, 2016, p. 112) was created as parental anxieties ballooned. The *need* to be anxious has been steadily fed to American parents since the 1980s with an increasing public emphasis on – *but not actually an increasing prevalence of* – child abductions, missing children, sexually exploited children, and the various dangers of leaving your child unsupervised (Brooks, Heywood, Mintz, and Senior all write about this well-documented trend). Our nation's attention turned to stranger danger and razorblades in Halloween candy. Intoxicated throughout the twentieth century by the capacity to shape our children's lives through birth control, vaccines, modern medicine, and an age-appropriate childhood, we bought the narrative that we could, in fact, prevent our child from ever experiencing any danger. We just had to watch out – always. And if something tragic did befall our child, it was *our fault as the parent*. We grew more protective and more fearful. Contextually speaking – parents had fewer children per family, often only one or two, and a newfound capacity to monitor and preserve their children's health and well-being – the life of each child became more precious and guarded. The potential for danger became seemingly removable if only the adult could maintain constant supervision over everything their child did.

And that is exactly what has been attempted – the steady encroachment of adult control and supervision into every inch of a child's life in a historically unprecedented manner. Imperial childhood was born.

As if that wasn't enough, the safety of their children was not the only thing parents had to be worried about. Within the same parenting generation, the country's national security and economic prosperity was also framed through the prism of how parents raised children. Parents, teachers, and policy makers were told to be concerned about educational attainment, international comparisons, and the ability of schools to produce a competitive workforce – and to place these burdens on our children, to insert them into their daily lives. *A Nation at Risk: The Imperative for Educational Reform* was published in 1983 by the National Commission on Excellence in Education (a mere century prior, graded public schools were still in their infancy) and argued that American students were falling behind their international peers and painting a devastating picture of the country's economic future if we let this continue any longer. This was a landmark document and it's sentiment continues to reverberate in schools and policy circles 40 years later. Lines like these continue to hold sway over our country's perspective on education:

The educational foundations of our society are presently being eroded by a rising tide of mediocrity that threatens our very future as a Nation and a People. What was unimaginable a generation ago has begun to occur– others are matching and surpassing our educational attainments. If an unfriendly foreign power had attempted to impose on America the mediocre educational performance that exists today, we might well have viewed it as an act of war…

The time is long past when American's destiny was assured simply by an abundance of natural resources and inexhaustible human enthusiasm, and by our relative isolation from the malignant problems of older civilizations. pp. 9–10

This sentiment is why the textbook on play at Fordham began with the statement that "the stakes are enormous" – children need to hit specific benchmarks or our country's future is in jeopardy. This has had a very real impact on the status of education and the role of schools. In the decades that followed, this would be felt in early childhood through the newfound belief in the efficacy of preschool in preparing children not only for kindergarten but also for a successful academic trajectory, a higher lifelong earning potential, and a more stable adult life. "Kindergarten readiness" became the watchword (an alien concept just a century ago). Early childhood was oriented away from its origin as a place to provide care for children while their parents worked (the legacy of the Industrial Revolution, smaller families, and working mothers) and began to focus on educational attainment and economic production (the legacy of scientific childhood and anxious parenting). Everything was elevated. Learning was not simply learning; it was weaponized to combat America's slipping international standards. Students were not just students; they were key to upholding our national "destiny." Play was not only play; it was a crucial tool in enhancing the country's power.

Neverland was taken away from children and replaced by scripted curricula and standardized tests.

Instructed to be worried about, and responsible for, their child's individual safety as well as the future of the country, parents became "uncritical consumers of anxiety," Brooks wrote. I stopped for a long while after I read those words. That phrase captured perfectly so much of the parenting I was seeing (a word cloud of my years in the field would have this phrase at the center in large letters). Brooks' *Small Animals* continues to be my go-to recommendation for bewildered parents unsure of how to navigate it all, which, to be honest, is basically every parent I've ever met (my copy is currently on loan to a preschool parent). I found Brooks' work so insightful, fresh, and impactful that I invited her in as the keynote speaker at a summer conference I was organizing at the time for Reggio-inspired preschool teachers; we gave a copy of her book to all attendees. She was tapped into the very real worry, stress, and anxiety I felt all around me from parents of young children, concerned that their child's, and nation's, future success hung on them making a sequence of hundreds of decisions correctly. Brooks marvelously un-spins this all and explores the social and cultural forces that have unwittingly convinced us that parenting equates to anxiety.

With parents trying to "control and ensure outcomes for their kids," this gave rise to the helicopter parents of the 1990s and their millennial successors of bulldozer, snowplow, and lawnmower parents (Lythcott-Haims, 2015, p. 5). Changing families, scientific childhood, and anxious parenting led to a curious new intervention into the daily lives of children. The "playdate" was invented in the 1980s – with fewer siblings at home to play with, parents fearful of leaving children unattended, and children's and parents' days more rigidly scheduled with school and work, the playdate emerged "as a practical scheduling tool (ibid, p. 3)." I'm pro-playdate! But the structuring of children's play under the watchful eyes of anxious parents (all of these were historically new social ingredients) had consequences: "once parents started scheduling play, they then began observing play, which led to involving themselves in play (ibid, p. 3)," which led to directing and supervising play: "unsupervised children were now unsafe children" (Brooks, 2018, p. 89). Parents and children (when not in preschool) were glued together in conspicuous fashion, locked in a never-ending dance of supervision and mandatory expectations.

I opened the 2018 preschool year using Kim Brooks (her book had just come out that August) as inspiration for my remarks at Parent Orientation that September:

As Brooks points out, we have succumbed to a cultural parenting paradigm in which our fear and anxiety overwhelm our warmer, softer instincts. Fear and anxiety drive us to over-parent, to worry, to care so deeply about each and every one of the millions of details that produce a child's life. This fear far too often winds up governing our parenting and our schools. We have been led to believe, through a devilish combination of developmental psychology, consumer marketing, and relative affluence, that if we can only make the "right" decisions as parents, we can control our children's path through life – we can ensure a good outcome. The unspoken converse of this is that we are then silently judged and critiqued when we make the "wrong" decisions. We drift towards control because we are fearful of being judged as a parent of an out of control child.

This has all created an "intensely American...parenting orientation" which is "a fundamentally anxious endeavor that require[es] planning and control at every level," leading to a "landscape of competitive, intensive, hypercontrolling parenthood" (Brooks, 2018, p. 47). Unsurprisingly, this yields a "hyperorganized, micromanaged" (ibid, p. 85), "overscheduled, checklisted childhood (Lythcott-Haims, 2015, p. 150)" in which "too many of us do some combination of overdirecting, overprotecting, or over-involving ourselves in our kids' lives (ibid, p. 7)." Six months after I gave those remarks to open the 2018 school year, the "Varsity Blues scandal" broke, in which dozens of parents paid millions of dollars to bribe and cheat their way through the college admissions process for their children, bringing this "intensely American" parenting approach into national headlines. Those parents implicated in the scandal are but the most exaggerated version of the cultural paradigm that breeds an imperial childhood.

"We're doing harm" (Lythcott-Haims, 2015, p. 8) (eek!) as a controlled childhood leads to children who are "underconstructed" and "existentially impotent" (ibid, p. 6). It was in this same stretch of time – the past 50 years – that parenting became an active verb, "something one could *do* all day long (Senior, 2015, p. 152)," breeding a type of "narcissistic" (p. 142) parent. This "hyperparenting" (ibid, p. 123) led to "the era of the protected child" (ibid, p. 176) which quickly became the "useless child" (ibid, p. 126) as children, who until recently had been contributors to the economy of the family, now became essentially inert vessels in which information and skills were deposited to be used at some distant point in the future when they would finally be allowed to enter mature community activities.

Children went from being active contributors to being stale objects of control. Within this new breed of narcissistic parenting, "how our kids look, what they eat, how they dress, what activities they pursue, [and] what they achieve have become reflections of us. Of how we see *ourselves*. Like *their* life is *our* accomplishment"

(Lythcott-Haims, p. 124). Fass sums this up succinctly when she writes that these factors have combined to create a paradigm in which parents are "eager to be as much in control as possible" in their children's lives: "It is the striving for control ... that differentiates family life today from...one hundred years ago" (2015, p. 220).

By the late 2010s, the box of being two had been built and imperial childhood had taken hold. These intertwining historical threads – some developing over centuries and others only more recently – led to a completely and radically transformed childhood by the time I met Emily in 2017. Today's childhood is thoroughly and scientifically described and normed, sealed off from adult society through preschool, segregated by discrete age bands, and imperialistically governed by the anxious whims of narcissistic parents. Children are offered a sanitized, useless childhood.

(*Remember, don't put the book down!*)

But. And there's a huge but.

Emily mattered! She didn't just sit back and accept the box of her imperial childhood. Children never have. Always striving, always resisting, she embodied Stetsenko's transformative activist stance. Human agency is a force which "can never be denied" even "from the first days of life" (2017, p. 349) in a process which "begins already in early childhood" (p. 283). Borrowing Stetsenko's words here, Emily's agency was modest, local, and mundane: agency can be felt "in *modest* ways and merely on *local* scales" (p. 182), "even seemingly *mundane* events...are starkly agentive and transformative" (p. 220), and "activist contributions...always matter (if only on a small scale) and typically, in *modest* ways" (p. 259). Due to their size and position within society, children are not capable of grand revolutions. But they are capable of small, local acts of agency, showing their powerful resistance through the means available to them.

Children may be small, but they are not trivial.

Despite the historical trends, Emily's transformative resistance made sure that the box of being two was not automatic or given. It was not to be her be-all and end-all. She would have a say. She would not let it define her.

References

Ariès, P. (1962). *Centuries of childhood: A social history of family life.* Knopf.

Brooks, K. (2018). *Small animals: Parenthood in the age of fear.* Flatiron.

Chudacoff, H. P. (2008). *Children at play: An American history.* NYU Press.

Cole, S. (2005). *To be young in America: Growing up with the country 1776–1940.* Little, Brown and Company.

Corsaro, W. A. (2011). *The sociology of childhood* (3rd ed.). SAGE Publications.

Dahlberg, G., Moss, P., & Pence, A. (2007). *Beyond quality in early childhood education and care: Languages and evaluation* (2nd ed.). Routledge.

Fass, P. (2016). *The end of American childhood: A history of parenting from life on the frontier to the managed child.* Oxford University Press.

Formanek-Brunell, M. (1993). *Made to play house: Dolls and the commercialization of American girlhood, 1830–1930.* Yale University Press.

Frost, J. L. (2009). *A history of children's play and play environments: Towards a contemporary child-saving movement.* Routledge.

Heywood, C. (2001). *A history of childhood: Children and childhood in the West from medieval to modern times.* Polity.

James, A., & James, A. (2004). *Constructing childhood: Theory, policy, and social practice.* Palgrave, Macmillan.

Kornei, K. (2020, October 23). Footprints mark a toddler's perilous prehistoric journey. *The New York Times.* https://www.nytimes.com/2020/10/23/science/ancient-footprints.html

Lythcott-Haims, J. (2015). *How to raise an adult: Break free of the overparenting trap and prepare your kid for success.* Henry Holt and Company.

Mintz, S. (2006). *Huck's raft: A history of American childhood.* Belknap Press.

NCHS 2011. Kirmeyer, S. E., & Hamilton, B. E. (n.d.). *NCHS data brief, number 68, August 2011.* Childbearing Differences among Three Generations of U.S. Women. https://www.cdc.gov/nchs/data/databriefs/db68.pdf

NCHS 2002. Matthews, T., & Hamilton, B. E. (n.d.). *Mean age of mother, 1970–2000. December 2002.* Mean Age of Mother, 1970–2000. https://www.cdc.gov/nchs/data/nvsr/nvsr51/nvsr51_01.pdf

NCHS 2023. Osterman, M. J., Hamilton, B. E., Martin, J. A., Driscoll, A. K., & Valenzuela, C. P. (2023, January 31). *National vital statistics reports.*

Births: Final Data for 2021. https://www.cdc.gov/nchs/data/nvsr/nvsr72/nvsr72-01.pdf

Rogoff, B. (2003). *The cultural nature of human development.* Oxford University Press.

Senior, J. (2015). *All joy and no fun: The paradox of modern parenting.* Echo.

Shinn, M. W. (1900). *The biography of a baby.* Houghton, Mifflin and Company.

The National Commission on Excellence in Education (1983). *A nation at risk: The imperative for educational reform.* United States. The National Commission on Excellence in Education.

The NCES fast facts tool provides quick answers to many education questions (National Center for Education Statistics). National Center for Education Statistics (NCES) Home Page, a part of the U.S. Department of Education. (n.d.a). https://nces.ed.gov/fastfacts/display.asp?id=516

The NCES fast facts tool provides quick answers to many education questions (National Center for Education Statistics). National Center for Education Statistics (NCES) Home Page, a part of the U.S. Department of Education. (n.d.b). https://nces.ed.gov/fastfacts/display.asp?id=4

3

The Daily Life of a Two-Year-Old

Emily's Life

In Emily's life, there was always a sheriff.

In today's hyper-surveilled, imperially controlled childhood, adult rules and expectations dominate the landscape of childhood. Because of this, just being herself – she was smart, verbal, volitional, eager, social, polite, energetic, and curious – often meant pushing back against the constraints of being two. Connecting an ethnographic portrait of Emily's daily life with a historical understanding of contemporary childhood, I realized that the simple act of voicing her mind became an act of protest.

Emily's voice became one of resistance.

Emily was not a particularly stubborn child. She was not noticeably more resistant than her peers. Her dissent was casual and commonplace, almost never exaggerated beyond what her peers frequently displayed. It fits easily into the landscape of childhood I was familiar with from my experiences as a teacher, director, and parent. Nothing I saw Emily do, or the circumstances she was in, felt out of the ordinary. Kate thought back on our time together and told me in my final field observation, "I feel like you got to see a lot of our normal rigamarole. Like, we didn't really do anything unusual." Exactly what I was after – the normal, mundane life of a two-year-old.

DOI: 10.4324/9781003455929-3

Emily at School

Cantaloupe and milk were on the menu for snack on a typical day in February and the children were scarfing them down. But tensions were rising as the sheriff – Michelle, in this case – strained under the weight of Emily and her outlaw band of classmates. Law and order were breaking down. A child's milk spilled on the table and rather than clean it, the child licked it up (I promise you, this happened).

You're getting dropped in mid-scene here, so let me give you some context. Things were not going as planned. The Little Ones were already behind schedule for the day. Yasmin and Tanya were both taking care of other responsibilities, leaving Michelle as the lone teacher at the snack table. Not an enviable position to be in, given the control she was expected to maintain over the 11 children clamoring for more, more, more! She had taken care to remind everyone as snack began: "We're having snack and then David's gonna come." David was a class favorite, visiting Little Ones each week for a lively music session. But he arrived each week at 10:20am, leaving the class with a quicker morning pace – they had to clean up from play time at 10am instead of their usual 10:30am.

Outmanned and outgunned, Michelle seemed exasperated.

Just prior to snack, at 10:04am, the classroom timer had rung (the timer was always disrupting Emily's life!). The teachers called out, "Time to put our toys away!" Usually sing-songy at clean-up time, the teachers were in a rush today to keep their schedule, having already missed the 10am cleanup deadline. Emily, as usual, was plain-spoken in her resistance: "No! I'm not putting this away. I'm not putting the toys away." Stetsenko taught me that agency is not a shadowy, vague force – it is "a this-worldly process" (2017, p. 206), by which she means that it is enacted by humans in their social interactions – it is something you can see happen. And here it was, happening right in front of me. As frustrating as it would be to her teachers, this was Emily acting with volition, with agency, and it would typically begin with that most powerful weapon of hers – "No!".

As her peers began to clean up, she repeated herself softly to no one in particular, "No! It's my toy. I don't want to put it away." These are the lines that I would have missed as a teacher. Sticking closely with one child, a clearer picture comes out as to how these transitions and attendant expectations are experienced. Tanya came over to enforce the expectations – what the adults expected her to do – and assist Emily in meeting them. They joined the hum of the class and carefully put a few puzzle pieces back in the box. Bodies and toys were in motion as the class re-set for snack time. Emily clung tightly to her toy.

At 10:15am, things settled down, and Emily sat at the snack table with her peers. A disposable paper cup, like the kind you use at the dentist's office to rinse your mouth out with, was placed in front of her, filled with chunks of cantaloupe, alongside a cup of milk. Emily had last eaten at 8:00am, a frozen pancake in her stroller as they left the apartment (Kate told me at 7:20am, as the girls were getting dressed, "Everybody woke up super early, this is like the middle of their day!"). After a long morning at home and a busy morning in the classroom, Emily was hungry. Like her classmates, she finished the fruit quickly and wanted more. But Michelle was solo and knew that David was entering the classroom in just 5 minutes. His timing could not be delayed.

The snack table was lively, the energy flowing. The 11 Little Ones encircled one table; some sat, some stood, all jostled. I wrote in my fieldnotes, "the children are cacophonous, vibrant, and giggly; lots of peer giggle and jovial chatter." By 10:18am (things happen quickly in preschool!), the cantaloupe cups were all empty and the requests were piling up from around the table. Here they are, with Michelle's responses in italics:

I want more.
Can you sit in your chair? [Children had to sit if they were to eat; this was a firm rule in Little Ones]
No, no, Michelle, I want more.
You want more?
Yea.
I want more.
I want more.

I want more.
I want more cantaloupe.
No, more!
I'm getting you some melon. Can you sit in your chair?
I want more cantaloupe.
Can I have some more cantaloupe? [Here is Emily, for the first time]
Can I have some more cantaloupe?
I'm going to serve you.
Can I have some more cantaloupe? [Emily again. So polite!]
Can I have some more cantaloupe?
And me! And me! And me!
Yes, I'm going to serve you some.
I want milk, too.
I want milk!
I want milk, too.

The next 45 seconds were a messy preschool blur – a scheduled transition, a blitz of motion, and lots of student resistance. This is where it is so helpful to have the ethnographic data – the audio transcription and fieldnotes – to slow things down and capture the full scene. At 10:20am, Yasmin entered the classroom and proclaimed to all, but with a raised eyebrow pointed toward Michelle: "So, David is here, are we ready for David?" A quick eyeball of the classroom gives the obvious answer – definitely not ready! It was clear that the children wanted more food and were, to be frank, having an absolute blast at the snack table.

But Michelle was the sheriff, and so this was her call. I've been there as a teacher, and I would have made the same call.

I didn't have a problem with it when I was a teacher. I do now.

"Yeah, we're ready."

I thought to myself, *What? No way! Not yet!*

This is how children are turned into outlaws – when we rate their behavior against adult expectations. This is how requests turn into protests. This is how agency turns into resistance. Native culture is outlawed as imperial control takes root.

"Let's finish!", one of Emily's classmates piped up. Yasmin was confused – "what?" – and so the student clarified her protest: "Let's finish milk." Yasmin blew through this and said to the whole group: "So, yeah, if you're ready, let's go sit on the rug." Yasmin and Michelle sang together, *"Let's make a circle, circle, circle."* Just like during clean-up time – a mere 16 minutes ago – Emily protested. Again. "No! I'm not done!"

There it was: the soundtrack to my time with Emily. When adults extended control into Emily's life, her agency was visible through her dissent. I considered Emily's audacity – her tremendous capacity to defy her teachers despite their obvious position of authority – and thought back to Stetsenko, who wrote that human agency comes through even in the bleakest of moments, "regardless of how powerless and oppressed, seemingly insignificant and fragile this one person may appear to others or even to oneself" (2017, p. 216). Emily protested. Against all odds.

Yasmin crouched down – her teachers were each unfailingly gentle and kind – and calmly told her, "Emily, David is here. But if you want, later when he leaves, we can give you a little more, alright?" David had indeed arrived. It was 10:21am.

Emily wasn't done playing but it was time for snack, so Tanya helped make sure she followed the rules.

Emily wasn't done with snack but it was time for music, so Yasmin helped make sure she followed the rules.

The sheriff and the outlaw. Rules and resistance. Teaching means controlling children. To speak up is to resist.

Carla Shalaby captures this sentiment in her thunderous 2017 book, *Troublemakers: Lessons in Freedom from Young Children at School*:

> The demands of school seem increasingly antithetical to how children be in the world. They move and run and jump and skip; they do not sit still for long stretches. They learn to do new things – crawl, talk, walk – when they are ready, not when adults decide they should be ready. And though dependent on caretakers, young children eagerly seek and exercise autonomy. They tirelessly refuse, protest, and question. *No* and *why* are the favored

words of little ones. School does not welcome this protest. Everyone is at the ready to catch children doing the
wrong thing. Unquestioning deference to authority is the
requirement and expectation of school, where adult dir-
ectives replace children's own desires.

Introduction, xxvi

Ouch. It's not pretty but it's what I came to see in Emily's life.

Emily's teachers were quite gentle and always kind – most
preschool teachers are! – but they couldn't escape the imperial
relationship. It's baked into the classroom model; it's how we
train our teachers.

Michelle took care to explain to me during an interview that she
seeks "shared power" with the students to avoid the feeling of (she
used an exaggerated voice of authority for this, sounding perhaps
like Papa Bear from Goldilocks), "I'm the teacher and I'm sitting
there on my big chair" (an ironic phrase, given the fact that the
teachers *did* sit on the big chairs). It was always a back-and-forth for
her, though: "We *are* the teachers so there is obviously always gonna
be that." She continued exploring the tension she felt, the same
tension that spurred this quest of mine, in balancing out respect for
the child's individuality with her need as a teacher to be in control:

> We technically do whatever we want, right? They are in
> our control, right? I would never want to be that teacher
> where I am projecting how I'm feeling or like be the rule-
> enforcer… You struggle with that safety line, and if a child
> is not listening to you – how you should handle that…
>
> It's just that balance, when you really need the child
> to do what you're asking, or you have to think about: Is
> this coming from me, what I want them to do, not neces-
> sarily what they want to do or what they need to be
> doing? Why does she need to be sitting when I give her a
> high five? I want her to be, but it's coming from what you
> want versus what she wants.

Ultimately, Michelle settled on "giving them a sense of
control or choice but still holding that role [as a teacher with

control]." Yasmin agreed, stating that when it comes to controlling children:

> It's so tricky! It's kind of hard. I mean, they are little individuals. They are humans just like us, and I think sometimes we forget that. I think a lot of times as adults we think that we can control these little humans, because they don't know everything yet. You know? But at the same time, they are so smart, they pick up on everything. And they have feelings. And they have knowledge. You know?

I know!

With Michelle's sensitivity to being "the rule-enforcer," and Yasmin's hesitancy to "control these little humans," why did they need to end snack and begin music?

In a surveilled, age-graded preschool classroom, it's all about the schedule. The clock dictates all.

At school, the 11 Little Ones napped together from 12:00 to 1:50 pm. Getting to nap on time meant keeping a schedule. Everything sort of worked backward from there. Lunch needed to start by 11:30am, which was preceded by a quick half hour on the rooftop playground. This left the morning – about 2 hours, from drop off until 11am, for everything else: free play, snack, meeting, music, and any other activities. I know this to be true in essentially every preschool classroom – first, the major parts of the day like eating and sleeping are plugged in, then come specials like music, art, or sports, which are added based on when the specialist is available (never based on when would be most appropriate for, or appreciated by, the children), and finally the rest of the child's day is filled in with play time or other activities. The box is built. But it's an ill fit that requires far too much *smushing*.

The tricky part is that in a classroom, this has to all happen at the same time, for everyone, always. Remember that preschool – and the constraints of the preschool schedule – is not a biological necessity but rather a (very recent) cultural invention. We do this *to* children.

Invariably, this meant that the children's play was interrupted by the teachers in order to move them along. This is why Emily needed to clean up at 10:04 am and finish snack at 10:20 am. So that when music ended, she could go to the roof and still be back in time for lunch, then rest, then pick up. Unless Emily's needs, wants, and desires matched this timing perfectly, which of course they never did, she was left with two options: submit or resist.

This was the axis on which her relationship with adults rested.

On a typical morning as the children were busy in their play, Yasmin announced to the class, "We're going to put a timer on for five minutes," which Michelle quickly followed up with the reminder, "Little Ones, we have five more minutes left to play." This began to make less and less sense to me. Never were the children slowing down on their own, showing the teachers they were ready to stop. It was always because of the schedule, never because of the children. The teachers set the dial on their old school kitchen timer, and Yasmin followed up after it went off: "Did you hear that? The timer went off and it's telling us it's time to, (Singing) *Clean up, clean up, everybody everywhere, clean up, clean up, everybody do your share.*" Emily, busy at the water table this morning, didn't look up. This happened so frequently that she knew what to expect next. Here came Yasmin, flashing her sheriff badge: "I'm closing the water table, okay Emily? Emily, we need to head over to the block area [to clean up] and I'll be right next to you, okay?"

The drumbeat was always the same:

Little Ones, we have five more minutes left to play. Five more minutes. I'm going to set the timer for five minutes.
Little Ones, we have two more minutes until clean up, two more minutes.
Time to clean up. *Clean up, clean up, everybody everywhere, everybody do your share.*
OK Little Ones, it's time to clean up. *Clean up, clean up, everybody everywhere, clean up, clean up, everybody do your share.*

I asked the teachers to walk me through Emily's time with them so I could better understand these transitions. We started from the beginning of the day. Michelle said Emily "definitely like, walks in, owning the place" – they all laughed in agreement, with Yasmin adding, "she's definitely confident when she walks right through the door." Yasmin explained that "it's free time" at drop off and Tanya said, "she likes to paint first" (just like Zoe!). After painting, Michelle said, "she visits a lot of areas. I think the area that I've seen her stay in the longest is definitely dramatic play. And then I would say the water table, too. She likes to use her imagination." And then here it comes – the transition, the timer, the 5-more-minutes.

"After free time, we have cleanup," Michelle said. Tanya explained, "we give them time – like we would tell them, '*You have five more minutes; in five more minutes we start cleaning up.*' Any transition, at this age, we give them time. Never ever happens abruptly. We go to each and every child and say, '*You have five more minutes.*'"

Note the use of age, again – the countdown was deemed age-appropriate; this fit inside the box – it was a strategy to assist in compliance, given the age of the child.

They kept going and walked me through the rest of the day. Each transition served to get the children to the next activity, with the overarching goal of napping at noon. This was all exactly what I did as a teacher and what is taught in early childhood textbooks – this is how it is supposed to be. The teachers had to get the timing of each transition right. That was their day. They had to be in control. That was their job. The problem was that the timing of the day – within a controlled childhood, essentially forced on the teachers and students by age-based segregation and developmentally appropriate practices – just wasn't the right match for all the children. But rather than flex to allow for divergence, the teachers needed to clamp down and control the children. This is not specific to Little Ones; this is a truism throughout preschool classrooms.

The imperial teacher – over-extending control into the life of a child, beyond what is obviously necessary for safety, always telling her what to do – was something Emily brought up repeatedly in our Duplo interviews. When she played the role of the

Duplo-teacher, there were always commands to be said (the teachers that Emily voiced in her Duplo play actually rarely said anything except commands):

> Ok! We have to go to nap time! If you're done with lunch, this is the nap.
> Remember – five more minutes – two more minutes – one more minute – Little Ones, TWO MORE MINUTES!
> I don't know why you need your coat – you just need your coat!
> No! No! You can't stand up, guys. Let's try this again, OK? You guys can't stand up, OK? OK? You have to listen, guys!
> He's not being safe. I'm gonna tell him he's not being safe. You need to be safe, OK? You need to be careful, or everyone will be sad, OK?

One afternoon on the living room rug, Emily assumed the roles of both her mom and herself. Hard to follow! I had to review the audio and my fieldnotes a few times to get this one right. In the interview, it was pickup time at our pretend school and Emily took her Duplo-Emily and slumped her over sadly toward Duplo-mom, owning both voices:

Duplo-mom asked sad-Duplo-Emily: What happened?
Duplo-Emily: Somebody couldn't let me stand up during lunch time.
Duplo-mom: Well, you have to listen to your teachers.
Duplo-Emily: But they say, 'No, you can't stand up'.
Duplo-mom: Listen to your teachers, OK? You have to keep sitting down.

I see this on repeat as parents and teachers drift toward each other and embrace each other's perspective on any given subject, often at the expense of the child's perspective. Emily knew that her mom would back up the teachers rather than empathize with her cause. This mirrors the collaboration Emily saw between Michelle and Yasmin during the cantaloupe fiasco –

adults always back each other up, passing the baton of control from one to the next. This happened regularly. On another day, Emily abandoned her clean-up duties, leaving her blocks on the floor instead of putting them away. Michelle walked toward her and began to pick the blocks up, but Yasmin, who had been watching and also walked over, told Michelle: "Don't pick them up." Michelle backed away, leaving Yasmin to complete her instructions to Emily and hold her accountable: "I saved these blocks for you. I can help you: you put one away, I'll put one away. I know you don't want to, but we need to." As adults we check in with each other, rarely allowing the child's voice to have relevance. Emily noticed that.

From the child's perspective, the adults in their life coordinate and collaborate in their pursuit of control (even the really nice ones!). Children know this: the parents' job is to reinforce the teachers' expectations (and vice versa), rather than appreciate and consider the child's perspective. This is where I kept seeing the box of being two as "inescapable" – as lovely and kind as her teachers and parents were, she had no ally in her resistance – other than her classmates, who were always up for banding together – no one to say, "Wow, it must be hard having people tell you what to do all day! I know how much you love to move. Maybe we can figure out how you can move around a little more when you need to during lunch time." Or what if Michelle replied to Yasmin, "Yes, I agree it is important for Emily to learn to clean up. But today, I'm going to give her a little break and do it for her." Do we need to default to the adult collaborator, every time? Can we ever ally ourselves with the young child? Even just … sometimes?

Stetsenko pointed me toward Marx Wartofsky, a philosopher who focused on historical epistemology (*a fascinating field that explores how knowledge is created through cultural practices – or in our case, how we developed our modern understanding of childhood*). Emily's internalization of the imperial teacher reminded me of his forceful writing, as he makes the claim that cultural practices like the science of child development and the preschool classroom are "nervous attempts to conceive childhood in terms of what we can contain and control" (1983, p. 200). Embedded in Emily's life, this claim – that would have felt outlandish to me as a classroom teacher – now made sense. Yes, actually, I could see it plainly in front of me, how teachers use the classroom as a space to "contain and control" children and childhood. I went back to Cannella (the book I put down out of frustration earlier in my time at Teachers College) and, this time, nodded along as she wrote, "child development is actually a covert method for social control and regulation" (1997, p. 61). Yes.

It started to click. It's all out there in the open yet there is a covertness to it – yes, learning, growth, and development are wonderful parts of early childhood but, no, an intense emphasis on control is not necessary to accomplish these goals. We glorify the truly wonderful parts of preschool (of which there are many!) but brush under the rug the difficult parts such as how on earth to convince all the children to do the same thing at the same time while also respecting their autonomy, their differences, and their agency.

On my very last visit with Emily, I noticed that the teachers moved the three main toy shelves during lunchtime to form a perimeter around the circle rug where morning meeting took place. It looked like they had circled the wagons to shield against a band of … you guessed it, outlaws. But at first, I couldn't figure out what this was, so I asked Tanya, who was seated next to Emily as usual. She explained, "it's a different setting we're trying" during lunchtime "because – the kids get so wild – moving around – just running around." Apparently, the children were eloping from lunch to the rug to read and play (such a crime!). This interfered with the schedule. The Little Ones had to eat during lunch, not play, or how would they nap on time? So the teachers moved the shelves to keep the children off the rug and in their seats.

Well, Emily took her agency and smashed through the perimeter. She eloped alright, as did a number of children, bopping back and forth from their lunch seats to the toy shelves, followed by repeated admonitions from Tanya to "sit on the chair" and "sit down." Again, the teachers' expectations made certain that Emily's urge to *move* could *only be expressed* as resistance. Just several minutes after Tanya explained to me why they had moved the shelves, my fieldnote reads: "at this point the children are using the shelf as a gate, going in and out of the rug area. Completely subverted the teachers' goal with the furniture."

It was time for me to go, and this would be my parting image of the Little Ones: Emily and her pals, frolicking to and fro. Agency has its perks.

Emily with Mom

Adult control continued at home. Dressed and ready for school, we were about to leave Emily's apartment. Emily was hoping to walk to school today, a length I'd seen her walk twice already – a full mile on her own two feet, imagine that! – but only on the way home, when there were no deadlines to meet. As Kate described it, "She walked all the way home yesterday" because "we didn't have to go to Susan's school [for pickup]".

But today, school was waiting, and so Emily had the wrong idea. Kate, to be fair, was no gunslinger. Just like the teachers, she was sweet and kind, gentle and patient; to be plainspoken, I thought the world of her as a mom and admired the intention and love that she brought to her relationships with her daughters. Emily had the good fortune of being surrounded by adults who loved her and showered her with positive emotions. But like it or not, this was an imperial childhood, and right now Kate had the shiny sheriff badge on her chest.

Mom was always in charge. And Emily was always resisting.

Like Yasmin, Kate wore her authority as gently as she could, offering Emily a chance to walk from the apartment door to the elevator down the hall and then through the lobby before getting in the stroller: "You can say hi to Norman (the doorman) and then you're gonna hop in the stroller." With that, we left the apartment, Emily on her own feet for just a little longer. This back-and-forth happened every morning and by now Emily knew this was a lopsided compromise:

Emily: Mom, I want to walk all the way.
Kate: No, you're gonna walk downstairs, say hi to Norman, and then you're gonna get in the stroller.
Emily: Then I'm gonna walk outside.
Kate: No, you're not gonna walk all the way.

Another time as they left the house:

Kate: OK when we get outside, we're going to get in the stroller.
Emily: No.
Kate: Yes.
Emily: No!
Kate: We're going to say hi to Jimmy, and then we're going to get in the stroller when we get outside, ok?
Emily: No, no. I want to walk! Can I walk for a little bit?
Kate: Not this morning.

And another day, by now you know what to expect, just like Emily:

Kate: Okay when we get outside, we're going to get in the stroller.
Emily: No.
Kate: Yes.
Emily: No, it's not a long walk!!
Kate: Oh?
Emily: It's – it's a short walk!
Kate: We're going to say hi to John, and then we're going to get in the stroller when we get outside, okay?
Emily: No. No. It's a close walk.
Kate: It's not a close walk.
Emily: I want to walk!

On one uneventful winter afternoon, Kate and Emily left the apartment with Susan to drop her off at an afterschool activity, came back in between, then left again to get Susan, which meant two round-trip schleps in the stroller. It was late, dark, and cold – Kate had all the reason to keep Emily bundled up in the stroller.

Emily didn't care much for those reasons, though. She wanted to move, as usual. Here are her collected comments from that walk, which sort of became the background noise and often went unanswered:

Emily: Can I walk a little bit?
Mom, don't buckle me.
Mom, can I walk?

Can I walk?
Mom, can I walk?
Can I walk?
Mom, can I walk a little bit?
I wanna walk.
Now can I walk?
Can I walk around there?
Can I walk?
Mom, can I walk?

The answer, of course, was no.

Each of these scenes ended the exact same way, with Kate hoisting Emily into the stroller and buckling her in. "Hoist" was a word that came up often in my data (at least once in nearly every visit), both at home and at school, a convenient way for adults to cut through Emily's resistance and move things forward. After all, the law is on the side of the sheriff (*do the ends justify the means?*). Once buckled, Emily would then strain forward, her upper body pulling against the five-point harness which locked her hips in place.

Captive. Straining. Sheriff. Outlaw.

This image captures much of Emily's life. I think about this now when I see a child push against the harness of their car seat or stroller, or worse, the buckle on their chair at preschool (yes, that is a thing), and I consider the backstory. How many times has this child resisted a transition already today? How many more to go? How many times have they protested being restrained? Being hoisted? Will they submit or continue to resist?

Nap time dominated the schedule at school, but would play second fiddle to other events at home as Emily's sleep was coordinated around the comings-and-goings of family life (*remember Lareau's concerted cultivation? "Organized activities, established and controlled by mothers and fathers, dominate the lives of middle-class children"*). Kate would inform her in the afternoon:

Clean up some things and then get ready for nap time.
We're gonna take an early nap today, 'cause we have to pick up
   Susan for school.
Stop playing with your toys, it's time for nap.

Don't go to sleep now, Emily. Don't go to sleep now 'cause we're gonna have some lunch and then go to Susan's school.

The same was true for Emily's morning play. Kate made for the kindest sheriff I've ever met, prodding Emily to keep pace each morning as they got ready to leave: "You only have thirty more minutes before leaving," "We're gonna leave in like ten minutes, OK?" "Five minutes and then we're gonna go." "It's time to go, remember? Five minutes." "That's not really a good thing to do before school because it takes a long time." "Oh no – no – we're not gonna do that, we're not dressing up before school." "No, Emily, we have to go."

Here is my very first school morning with Emily, in early September. It's the same scene described to me regularly by pre-school parents in my Coffee Chats, the same scene in my own home, and it would be the same scene nearly every morning for Emily:

Susan: C'mon, Emily!

Emily: I am – just give me a second! Just give me a second mommy! Mom just give me a second.

John: What are you doing Emily? It's time to go – remember?

Emily: I'm trying to -

John: You need to wrap up playing so you can go get your shoes on. OK Emily – five seconds. Where are your shoes?!

"Five seconds" would stretch into six minutes (it always does) as John, Susan, and Emily sort of danced around each other grabbing for a collection of shoes, keys, lunchboxes, and bags. Eventually ready to go, Emily looked up and said, "Mom, I want to walk ALL the way."

You already know how that would go.

There was always an adult telling Emily what she needed to do, how she needed to do it, and when it had to happen. It seemed exhausting. Not only for Emily but for the adults too. Keeping Emily on pace required diligence by her teachers or parents to always be "on." It reminded me of the line from Jennifer Senior's book that only recently had parenting become "something one could *do* all day long."

From the moment Emily got up until the moment she got dropped off at preschool, Kate was *parenting*. Which meant for the most part, and especially around transitions and expectations, telling Emily what to do. Shoes, hair, clothes, food, stroller: every single piece of the interaction came with expectations and resistance. Why do we do this to ourselves? Why are we stuck in this awful morning sequence in which we must convince our child to do something they do not want to do? I came back to Fass' observation that the recent creation of separate spheres for family, work, and school "reframed the parent-child relationship" in profound ways. Exactly! This is a cultural moment on repeat, the daily consequence of an imperial, age-banded childhood and the historical and sociological trends that got us here.

I talked to Kate and John about all this one evening after the girls were asleep – timing and transitions, how the family schedule fit together. I read back a transcript from one of the many morning scenes in which Kate and Emily tumbled toward the goal of leaving the house on time. I asked about scenes like this: "What decisions are you making? What is important to you in the moment?" Kate took a long pause before answering:

> So, there is a lot of things happening. So like, on any given day, usually we have to take Susan to school at a given time. And so, it's not free flowing. I usually get Emily ready, so that I can finish up and get Susan ready, so that we can get Susan to school on time, so that we need to get Emily to school on the earlier end. I like her to get there early because I think it's just easier to transition into the room when there's less kids there. So, I always try to get her there before 8:45.

We were getting closer: "To drill down on the obvious stuff, why do you feel compelled to get Susan to school on time? That's a priority that's driving a lot of this."

> We leave at 8:00 so that we can walk and do our thing and get there. And also, I'd like her to be early, because they are actually doing work during their arrival time. So, she could show up at like 9:00 every day but then she would miss a whole chunk. So, she goes early. And it like, kind of

sets up everybody's day. Plus, they get up early. And we live like basically 10 blocks from one school [Emily's] and five blocks from the other [Susan's]. I just like them to be early. Just in getting out the door, like as a family, I think we all realized, they eat first, get dressed, and then like brush their teeth, then you can use the rest of it as your free time to do whatever you want to do. If we let them just play in the morning, they wouldn't get to school until like 10:30. And I like to be early. I do. And for preschool there is an added benefit if you get there early because you get to have this whole interaction with your teacher, you can go to the bathroom without anybody else there... And I mean whatever, if you get there late, you get there late. But I don't like that to be our normal pattern. So.

So!

Just like in school, the schedule must be kept. The schedule, and what the sheriff understands the goals of the schedule to be, overrides the desire of the child who is shuttled *through* the schedule. It would seem preposterous to ask the child to design the daily schedule, right? I agree. But I think there ought to be a nuanced middle ground, a way that we could do a better job of simply listening to and empathizing with young children during these moments when they protest the pace of transitions we push them through.

Maybe it's the transitions (having specific times when the young child has to leave home, clean the classroom, or end snack) and the expectations (sitting still at snack time, buckled into the stroller on the way to school) that are the problem, not the child's resistance to them. Are the ways that we insert these restraints and controls into children's lives fully necessary? Can we chip away at them, even a little?

Schedules kept interfering with the things Emily wanted to do.

Toward the end of October, we walked out of school with Yuval, Emily's classmate and new friend, and Stacy, his caregiver. Emily and Yuval had been spending a lot of time together at school and their friendship was growing right in front of us (the best gift preschool can give a child is a best friend). They held hands as they walked out of the school building; Yuval offered

Emily a bite of the muffin in his hand and she happily obliged. Emily, ever bold, was ready for more: "Mommy, mommy, tomorrow can I have a playdate with Yuval?" (*remember, invented a brief 40 years ago*).

I jotted down in my fieldnotes (always messy scribbles, walking behind the stroller), "This is a big move for Emily, lots of agency here, let's see how it goes!" In a romcom, you could cue up the sappy montage as they pursue each other. But these were children, and their lives were coordinated by adults:

Kate: Oh tomorrow?!
Emily: Yea. Tomorrow?
Kate: I need to look, I'm not sure what's going on tomorrow.
Emily: Me and Yuval – can -
Stacy: You want to have a playdate with Yuval?
Emily: Yea!
Stacy: [To Kate] We have to get Ori [Yuval's big brother].
Kate: I know! We both have to pick up other kids, it's hard to do it.

Kate and Stacy pulled out their phones to look at their calendars. They scrolled down to November. I'm reminded again of the "hyper-organized" (Brooks) and "overscheduled" (Lythcott-Haims) nature of imperial childhood:

Kate: Wednesdays are awesome for us because I don't have to pick up her older sister until 5:30.
Stacy: Mondays, both boys [Ori and Yuval] have something. Then I'm not here, Tuesday, Wednesday…the best is going to be to talk to Yuval's parents.
Kate: I'll text Yuval's mom and see what she says.

Kate turns to Emily, and I jot down that she is "sheepishly self-mocking" in her tone – she seemed to realize it was a bit silly that the kids couldn't just play:

Kate: Alright it's a complicated answer, Emily. We're working on it. We're working on a playdate, ok?
Emily: Today?
Kate: Definitely not today. But. Another time.

Emily and Yuval's budding friendship would continue to grow stronger throughout the year, but in this moment was cast aside by the constraints of an imperial childhood. There was too much going on in their lives for them to be allowed to play together that day or the next. The schedule was fixed, it was set; there is very little room in the young child's life to act with volition and seize the moment.

I understand that the lives of Emily's adults can't, and shouldn't, revolve around her every need and want. That is not my point or what I am advocating for, but to put it bluntly, Emily couldn't eat, play, sleep, or walk without someone, somewhere, telling her how and when to do it. Emily, and all young children, just need a bit more breathing room. There's got to be a time for the adult to just yield a little, loosen the standards, and accept that, every so often, the child's demands in that moment (to eat, to walk, to sleep, to play – these are basic, non-outlandish demands) can take priority over the schedule or the expectations.

Age-Based Segregation

In the histories reviewed in Chapter 2, I kept coming across the word "increasing" to describe age-grading and age-based segregation – as in, over the past century and a half, the presence of age-grading has gradually increased. After my time with Emily, I'm convinced we can now replace "increasing" with "fully saturated": Emily's life was fully saturated with age-based segregation. While this was most notable in Little Ones, I saw throughout the year just how profoundly this impacted everything she did. Keep in mind how historically unprecedented all of this is and consider that against the massive role it played in Emily's life.

Emily pined after the places her eight-year-old sister could go. I arrived one July morning as Kate was helping her daughters get ready for the day. Emily had on pink mermaid pajamas and was settled into the breakfast nook in the kitchen, eating her toast and ignoring her fruit and yogurt. She ate the toast straight down the middle, as if the goal was to separate the bread in half, and indeed left the two side chunks on her plate. As breakfast wound down, Kate mentioned: "It's almost time to take Susan to camp, ok?" Emily's eyes lit up: "Can I go to camp with Susan?" Mom stuttered for a second and I wrote down in my jottings that she "seems surprised, caught flat-footed" – reminiscent of how the teachers appeared when I asked them why the classroom was called Little Kids. Kate repeated the question: "Uh, can you go?" "Yea." "You can – come with me for drop off -" Kate began, but Emily finished the sentence to her liking: "– and then we can – and then I can go to camp." "Oh, you're not gonna go to camp yet," Kate replied, and deftly kept going, offering a Wonder Woman dress to Emily to wear for the day. The dress was attractive enough to Emily that she dropped the protest … for the moment.

We arrived in the lobby of the camp building and watched together – me, Kate, and Emily – as Susan ascended the stairs out of sight. Emily, never one to give up easily, looked up at her mother and pleaded, "Mom, can we go upstairs?" Kate, kindly yet firmly, answered the obvious truth that Emily knew was coming: "I think we're just gonna drop her off here." Emily protested, turning louder: "Mommy! I wanna – I wanna – I wanna – I wanna – mommy – I wanna go upstairs." "Well," Kate replied, always patient, "they're gonna go upstairs." "Mom, I want stairs." Kate ended the conversation: "Let's go home – you can finish your breakfast." A fellow camp-parent wryly glanced at Emily and then smiled at Kate, saying, "She's like, 'but I'm gonna miss choice time!'" Kate giggled politely. This would occur often throughout my time with Emily – an adult gently mocking Emily's attempts to escape the confines of her age-banded childhood.

We do this all the time – children do things that seem surprising to us because we think of them as an age instead of a person, so we laugh at them because it seems odd. I am so uncomfortable with it. We are the ones who decided it was odd, who standardized childhood and set it apart from the rest of society. And then we laugh at children when they have the audacity to be a part of something bigger than the box we place them in.

This all happened again the next month when Kate told me that "camp is over for Susan so now she's just having gymnastics." Emily, ever eager, initiated a rapid-fire ping-pong negotiation: "And I'm gonna do gymnastics!" Emily would repeat this demand every so often – to join her sister in gymnastics – even though it was denied when she first brought it up. This would happen often during my time with Emily, and I began to notice just how earnest she was with her proclamations. We tend to swat aside the random things they say because they don't really fit into our expectations. But I've learned that what adults think of as non-sequiturs or idle comments from children are often actually commitments that come with planning and follow-up. Kids mean what they say! I think there is room here for us to do a better job of *believing them* instead of always *denying them*. Mom was humorously incredulous – *people* do gymnastics, not *two-year-olds*: "You're gonna do gymnastics too?" "Yea!" "Mmmm we'll see-" "-and I'm gonna be on the team-" "-*you're* gonna be on the team?" "Yea!" Kate laughed gently and smiled at Emily.

When Kate did eventually sign Emily up for gymnastics, she explained to me, "it's not *really* like a class – more like open gym." I sat with Susan one afternoon as we watched Emily's "not really" class. Pointing to the children running around the gymnastics space, I asked her, "Is this the same as when you do it?". Susan rolled her eyes:

Susan: No way! We have REAL coaches.
Noah: Who's the lady here? [gymnastics staff member]
Susan: She's just watching them.
Noah: Ok so who are your coaches?
Susan: She's one of my coaches.
Noah: Oh, so she IS a coach?
Susan: Yea she's a coach.
Noah: But is she coaching right now?
Susan: No, she's not coaching, because they're just...being free. But for me, you have to stretch, run, like – they [pointing to Emily's group] just come in and play – we have to do, like, actual things, like floor, beam. They're just free – like they can do anything.

Emily never got to do the "actual thing." I could picture Susan with my copy of Rogoff's 2003 book, nodding along as she read:

> If young children cannot enter community activities, adults...design specialized child-focused settings for them. Adult-child play, lessons, and child-focused conversations seem to be a specific cultural solution to providing children with preparation for later mature contributions, while segregating them from participation during childhood. p. 149

This was confirmed again by the staff member who was "not coaching." I watched as Emily and her friends took some of the gymnastics elements – an arch and wedge meant for tumbling – and created a small fort for themselves to hide in. This looked like lots of fun and nothing like gymnastics. Shrieking deliriously, they tore down the structure and rebuilt it several times in a row. The "not coach" smiled as she looked at Kate and remarked, "I was gonna say something and then I was like, 'It's not real class! It's like, open gym time.' So -"

Emily's earnest plea from earlier rang in my head: "I'm gonna be on the team!" Here she was, with all the ingredients in place – on the gym mat, with the coach, ready for action – but her desire would be denied. She could play, she could be "free," she could "do anything," but she could not be on the gymnastics team – she was just two, after all. She was free as she explored the gymnastics space, but it was a Pyrrhic freedom (a victory tantamount to defeat – she gained access but could not actually *do* gymnastics) as the adults deemed this enough to satiate Emily's demand to join the gymnastics team. Early childhood requires that children play (freely, we ironically insist) and *only* play – at the cost of engaging in mature community activities, despite their repeated insistence for the latter.

Children want to be a part of the world in a way that age-based segregation unnecessarily prevents. They want, and deserve, more than the world we present to them.

Later in the year, Emily sat longingly outside Susan's door, not allowed to join a playdate happening inside: "The big kids are playing in there," Kate told her with a shrug. I asked if Emily was allowed in Susan's room when friends were not over and Kate explained, "No...it's like, there's so many little things in there...all of her toys are small" (Emily did sneak in quietly several times when Susan and Kate were not looking, of course. Sorry, Susan!). Again, it seemed exhausting. Emily could never escape the box, and Kate always had to enforce it – she needed to *parent*. There was always an adult, who always came with a rule.

A federal code called the "Small Parts Regulation" dominates the toys that young children are allowed to play with and holds enormous sway over the material culture of childhood. Published in 1980 in the Code of Federal Regulations (16 CFR, Sections 1500.18(a)(9), 1500.50–52; Office of the Federal Register, 2019; further specified in the Consumer Product Safety Commission's [CPSC] Age Determination Guidelines, Therell, 2002), the regulation calls to "ban certain toys intended for use by children under 3 years of age...because of small parts" (Therell, 2002, p. 1). This is why we have the warning on many toys, federally required since 1995 for any toy marketed to young children which contains a choking hazard: "WARNING: CHOKING HAZARD-Small parts. Not for children under 3 yrs." Place these regulations in the history of controlled childhood at the end of Chapter 2 – these regulations are emerging just as anxiety is spiking and control is ossifying. Every part of the child's life had to be controlled and regulated – for the safety of the child and the wellbeing of the country – and it was the parent's job to enforce this. Being under three, the ban had an interesting effect as Emily wound up barred from her sister's room – an unconceivable arrangement a century prior – because it *contained* small parts. Safety precautions around toy use have had the (perhaps) unintended effect of creating more no-go zones for young children, stretching the impact of age-based segregation. In the name of safety, children's interactions with the world are severely limited.

Sneaking in behind safety, and small parts, are the lingering effects of the problematic foundations of the scientific childhood reviewed in Chapter 2. In the name of child development, we maintain outdated ideas about children and what materials they can be allowed to use. We're stuck with this idea that *all* children of a certain age have the *same* interests and characteristics. We need to move on from this and nuance our perspective on what children can use and do, or at the very least, become aware of how this is massively restrictive in the daily life of a young child. In practice, it severely limits the world they are exposed to.

The same CPSC document reviewing small parts (CPSC Age Determination Guideline, Therell, 2002) also details how to distinguish what material is appropriate for what age group:

> Age labeling provides parents and other consumers guidance for selecting proper toys for children. CPSC staff, therefore, encourages age labeling. CPSC staff perform age determinations, in which the various characteristics of a toy are matched to the characteristics of children in a particular age group. For example, children from 12 through 18 months of age enjoy toys with bright colors, especially yellows and reds, and toys with high contrast and patterns. Therefore, toys with characteristics such as this may be considered as being intended for children of this age. pp. 3–4

It then outlines ten age groups that toys can be designated for (birth through three months, four through seven months, etc.), explaining that they are "modeled after developmental psychology, anatomy, and early childhood literature, particularly from the work of researcher Jean Piaget" (p. 7) – those titans of the scientifically defined childhood. This ignores the fact that a six-month-old can still enjoy, and benefit from, using a material labeled for two-year-olds (and vice versa). It ignores the fact that some children *are painters* and benefit from access to robust painting materials, not only child versions or what their developmental stage indicates they might prefer. Even more broadly, in practice, it convinces parents that their children should not interact with things that are not explicitly labeled as age-appropriate. Suddenly major portions of the child's life are off limits because they are not regulated. The world quickly becomes divided – *things my kid can do*, and *things they can't do*. Parents are under enormous pressure to get it right – to give their children the right things – and so these age determinations are often translated by the adults as scripture instead of guidelines. They become something to *enforce*.

The ways we understand children are still emerging and shifting. Our knowledge of who they are, what they can do, and what they want is not finalized; it never will be, since children, as humans, are cultural beings whose needs and wants *change along with the shifting culture they are a part of.* Developmental beliefs laid down a century ago should not define the parameters of today's childhood. In practice, age grading of toys tightly constrains the material culture of young children and severely limits the materials they are exposed to and allowed to interact with. Age-appropriate toys and materials offer children a closed, clean version of the world, one which presupposes and then reifies their abilities and interests.

I took a survey of the toys found in Emily's home and at school and found that, essentially, everything in her world was specifically for her age group:

Sampling of toys at school:

Zippers Buttons Bows by Moria Butterfield, "2-4 years"
Hexie Snaps by Popular Playthings, "For ages 2+"
Alphabet Outloud Talking Puzzle by Small World Toys, "2-5 years"
My First Matching Game by Ravensburger, "2-3yrs"
ABC Alphabet Building Blocks by Sarah Buel Dowling, "For ages 2+"
Circular Floor Puzzle Vehicle by Melissa and Doug, "Ages 2 and up"

Sampling of toys at home:

Mini Window Blocks by Guidecraft, "Ages 2+"
Santa's Christmas Set by LEGO DUPLO, "2-5" years
Stethoscope and Thermometer by BatTat, "3+" years
Standard Unit Blocks by Melissa and Doug, "3-8 years"
Clean Up Set by Melissa and Doug, "3-6 years"

The age grading of toys was intended to safely and accurately respond to children's interests by providing developmentally appropriate interactions. While it may accomplish those goals, what I observed in Emily's life is that the concept of age-grading of toys ultimately manifests in the real world as just another way for adults to control the child's exposure to the world.

This all extends well past toys, many of which are required to come with age labels, into non-regulated materials as well. One afternoon at home, Emily got a scrape and said, "maybe I'll put a band aid on, then I'll come back – I'm gonna get a band aid." As she went to her parents' bathroom, Kate replied, "Let's get some of your band aids, not daddy's." Kate returned with Crayon Bandages, which, according to a distributor's website, are "fun bandages...for kids. Kids will love the color variety" (Mountainside Medical, https://www.mountainside-medical. com/products, n.d., "Crayon Plastic Bandages," para. 1). Kate told me they are "less sticky" than John's band aids. Likewise, on another afternoon, Kate was packing up some shipping boxes. Emily asked, "Can I help with the tape?" Kate informed her, "No, not this tape, this isn't kid's tape." Kate's tape was kept in a closed cupboard which Emily did not have access to; the "kid's tape" is kept out on the children's art table and had a "plastic cutting edge for safety" (Walmart.com, n.d., "Description," para. 1) as compared to the metal cutting edge on Kate's tape.

Regular, everyday items in children's lives are swapped out for the child version which is a little less, a bit tamped down. The band aids are less sticky, the tape dispenser is less sharp. Children's scissors don't cut as well. Their forks and knives are dull. Their tools are plastic and only for pretending. Countless times each day, young children see adults using items that they are not allowed to access. Our desire for children to be safe, and to give them developmentally appropriate interactions, has radically shrunk the world that children are presented with.

Sometimes this is necessary. *Many* times, it is not.

I followed this line of thinking to help with another question about age that had popped up earlier in the research. Emily's family referred to the nearby playground as the "baby playground." When I asked Kate why, she explained it was because

"Susan's school doesn't play there." I searched for more answers. The playground was initially built in 1936 and pictures show one large, open space, presumably for a child of any age. However, it had been recently renovated, and the park website said it was now "geared towards pre-school-aged children" (this idea – "pre-school-aged children" – had not yet been invented in 1936). This meant the addition of "increased toddler swings" and the "creation of organized play experiences for 2- to 5-year-olds within the central zone of the playground" (Central Park Conservancy, 2016). This is why playgrounds are often segregated by age, typically with one area for 2–5-year-olds and another for 5–12-year-olds.

The CPSC *Public Playground Safety Handbook* (CPSC, 2015) sheds more light on what this means, with a section on "age separation" describing "age appropriate equipment" and mandating that "the landscaping of the playground should show the distinct areas for the different age groups" (pp. 6–7). This is mirrored by the New York State Department of Health's playground safety statement, which asks parents to "make sure your child uses age-appropriate equipment" and specifies that "children ages two to five should not climb higher than 60 inches" (NYS DOH, 2018, "What Playground Equipment," para. 1). That statement reflects a cultural belief and not a biological truth, an example of *sociocultural development*. The ways Emily was *allowed (forced?) to develop* came from cultural expectations.

150 years prior, before playgrounds were invented and then domesticated, before small parts were regulated, children – big and small – played together. Yes, Emily's apartment and playground were safer for all of these modern interventions. But everywhere I looked within Emily's life, every stone I turned over, I found age as a motivating factor for inserting more and more control into children's lives – children's social and built environment, it seemed, *must* narrowly reflect their biological age. In an imperial childhood, there is no alternative.

But Emily wasn't only an age – and one specific age did not accurately capture her life. Emily described herself throughout the research as variously "little," "a toddler," "a baby," "a little baby," "two," "a baby," "a bigger one," "just a toddler," "a Little

One," "not little," "not a toddler," "a big girl," "not a baby," and "a big kid." Sometimes, she absolutely detested being "little," as she made clear one morning at home when Kate placed a small slice of a peach in a bowl and handed it to her (I still laugh every time I recall this episode, seeing each of my children in this moment):

Emily: You put a little peach in here?
Kate: – and?
Emily: I'M NOT LITTLE! I don't need to eat a little peach!
Kate: You don't have to eat it.
Emily: This is a LITTLE PEACH!

But at other times she referred to herself as "small," such as an afternoon we spent climbing on the playground together:

Emily: Let's swing
[She gripped the trapeze bar and swung her body out below her.]
Noah: I can't really swing because my body is different than yours.
[I gripped the bar, but my longer legs trailed on the ground.]
Emily: I know, because mine is so small.
Noah: I'm very curious at what you just said – that your body is so small. Yesterday you told me that you don't use a pacifier because you're "not a baby", and that you do use the potty cause you're a "big kid" – so I'm a little confused – are you "small" or are you "big"?
Emily: Big. Because I'm not a baby.
Noah: How do you feel – do you feel big or small?
Emily: Um – small – cause I can't reach those.
[Points to an element on the playground structure beyond her grasp]
Noah: Mm-hmm.
Emily: Mm-hmm – cause I can just reach this [the trapeze bar] – I can reach this.

Despite our widespread adult insistence that children should be categorized by their age and presented with subsequently "age appropriate" opportunities (such as toys, playgrounds, and activities), this is not actually how children's lives unfold.

Pernille Hviid's work came to mind while dangling from the trapeze bar with Emily. Hviid is a psychology professor and researcher at the University of Copenhagen engaged in creative work around how children, families, and schools all interact. She writes that while adults imagine children as on a linear developmental journey – small to big, immature to mature, child to adult (kid band aids to daddy's band aids, kid tape to mommy's tape) – it is not necessarily experienced as such by the actual child. Interviewing five 12-year-old children about their memories from early childhood, the study found that "on many occasions the data twisted central and traditional understandings of human development. To the researcher's surprise, no child talked about development as a process where they felt bigger and bigger (2008, p. 186)." Instead, she finds that growth, size, and competency can instead be experienced by the child as paradigmatically fluid and contextual. Reflections from the children in Hviid's study produce a "zig zag" understanding of growth: as the prekindergarten year ends, they are "big" because they have grown in relation to the classroom setting and relative to the beginning of the year, and yet as the next school year begins, they are "small" again as they are placed in elementary school settings into which their bodies must now grow and where they see children much larger than themselves. The children report likewise feeling "small" while among their older siblings but "big" while on the playground with their peers.

Development is contextual. And the context of Emily's development was profoundly shaped by age-based segregation, which flattened and narrowed her world. Her appetite was larger than this world presumed – sometimes she wanted daddy's band aids! – and she often had to navigate being in a space, or using materials, or following expectations, that did not accurately match her self-image or capacity.

Nobody stopped to ask and listen – what did Emily want? What did she need? What was appropriate *for her*?

Infantilization

At pickup time one afternoon in the hallway outside of the Little Ones classroom, Kate reminded Emily that they were headed to a haircut after school. A mother overheard and asked where they were headed, to which Emily replied, "Kidville!" Both moms laughed as the mother commented, "Where else would you go!", and Kate replied, "Is there another option?!" (A Google search showed 20 hair salons within a ten-block radius; *people* have plenty of options but *two-year-olds* have only one tiny, little box). I asked Kate later about this – why is Kidville the only choice? It fits the box: "She's learned that a haircut means that you can watch a show, sit in the car (the barber chair was shaped like a toy car), and sometimes got a lollipop." For a two-year-old, that's a haircut.

Kate's description felt kind of familiar so later I combed my data to look for what this reminded me of. I found an example of basically the opposite scenario, as Kate was headed to the dentist one morning and Emily was to be left with a babysitter (and me!) in the apartment. Emily was tangling with her mom, begging to join her instead: "It won't be very fun; you'll just have to sit there." "Noooo I wanna go." "My dentist doesn't have a TV or toys or the treasure box, there's just magazines there." "No – noooo – mom I want to go with you to the dentist." "It's not gonna be a fun dentist. There's no TV, there's no prizes." The opposite of her mother's, Emily's dentist sounded just like Kidville, with TV and treats. The box was always the same: every interaction that Emily had with the world was mediated by the same interpretation of her being two.

Anyways, that afternoon we strolled from preschool to Kidville. We entered the shop just as a young girl climbed out of the chair with a lollipop in each hand. Bingo! Two-year-old-land! The hairdresser diverted Emily's focus away from the actual activity, asking her as she climbed into the car-chair: "All right, do you want to watch, um, Daniel Tiger?" Emily nodded yes and the hairdresser responded with dry irony, "How did I guess!" Her wry sarcasm matched the gentle mocking of the parent in the camp lobby and Kate's humorous incredulity about

Emily joining the gymnastics team. Adults had very narrow assumptions about who Emily was and just couldn't fathom her living outside of that box.

A few minutes later, as the hairdresser prepared to work on the back of Emily's head, she placed a small plastic bucket with a few toys in it on Emily's lap: "Oh my god, I have a question. Can you do me a favor? Can you look in this bucket? Do you see a zebra in there (at the bottom of the bucket)?" Emily muttered, "Yes." The hairdresser was working on Emily's neck, exposed while she looked down. "Oh, my goodness, you found it right away. Now look deep deep deep inside – do you see a horse? Look deep down in that bucket. Stay just where you are. Do you see the green frog? Good job, you can watch TV now." Moments later, the haircut was done. Emily hopped down and asked if she could have a lollipop. I learned later from Kate that this is what Emily should expect for several more years when she told me, "Susan just finally had her first haircut NOT in the chair."

As a young child, Emily was there to watch TV, look at toys, and eat lollipops. The box of childhood kept Emily cut off from learning about or participating meaningfully in, the activity itself. We know that learning occurs through participation – Rogoff (1990) has a whole theory about children learning through "apprenticeship" as they mimic the actions of the mature model, slowly absorbing and accruing skills and competencies. This requires *participation*, something age-based segregation disallows – recall again Cannella's searing line, that in a normed, controlled childhood, children are "isolated from the rest of the world and regulated through a controlled exposure" (p. 30). This kept happening – adults would isolate Emily from the actions needed to perform certain tasks, which would create a regulated, controlled exposure to the world around her – she was only allowed to do *certain things*, to participate in *certain ways*, while the rest was done *for her* or *to her*.

Contrast this with Rogoff's apprenticeship model in which the child engages with adults and mature tasks in meaningful ways from early on. She highlights how children in different cultural locations and historical eras have meaningfully participated and contributed in a variety of social, family, and economic settings. Recall Cole's line from Chapter 2, that children were "involved in almost all aspects of adult life" until relatively recently. Not Emily. Heywood describes how through "the desire to isolate children... from the world of adults, young people have been increasingly 'infantilized' by efforts to keep them out of the workplace...and to prolong their education in schools" (2001, p. 38). He describes this infantilization as similar to the gardening technique of grafting, in which material from one plant is inserted into a host plant so that the host comes to display the qualities of the new material. He writes that the infantilization I saw in Emily's life occurs as adults "take some fairly obvious biological feature of the age in question and graft on to it a series of more general qualities" (p. 40).

Emily was two, and two-year-olds have a "fairly obvious" biologically limited capacity. Developmentally appropriate practices graft onto this a more broadly helpless quality which ensures that the young child is removed from participating in any actions they are deemed incapable of. The quality of being helpless is grafted onto the young child.

Children can't do everything, so they're left doing nothing.

One day as lunchtime drew near, Emily walked to her cubby to get her lunchbox. She was surprised to see it wasn't there, so she went back into Little Ones, where Tanya basically took over and Emily's presence shriveled. Sometimes the messages we give children, usually without realizing it, are that they should just do nothing while we take care of everything. Because they are too young to know how to do it, and we know how to do everything, so we will do it for you.

Here is a typical lunch setup for Emily and a common scene in preschool classrooms, displaying the imperial relationship between the teacher and the child:

It was lunchtime on the Little Ones' schedule and so Emily walked to her cubby in the hallway just outside the classroom. She stood there next to her cubby, staring into her bag, confused as to why her lunchbox was not there. She knew it had been there earlier and couldn't figure out what had happened. At the same moment, Tanya was looking for Emily inside the classroom. After glancing around the classroom and coming up empty,

Tanya found Emily standing there in the hallway looking at her cubby. Tanya took Emily's hand and, the way a trainer might lead a horse, walked Emily to the spot at the lunch table where she had already placed the lunchbox. Then in one fluid motion, Emily sat down in her chair while Tanya opened her pasta container and poured the food out onto a paper plate. Emily started eating her pasta while Tanya held up a container of grapes and asked her, "Emily do you need me to help you with this?"; Tanya opened the container before Emily could respond. Still moving, Tanya placed a yogurt container and vegetable pouch in front of Emily: "Do you want this or this?" Emily mutely picked up the yogurt, which Tanya opened and placed back on the table. After a few minutes of eating, Emily stood up from the table and Tanya threw out the paper plate that had been filled with pasta.

This was typical of Tanya and Emily's interactions around lunch. On another occasion, Tanya unpacked the items in Emily's lunchbox, placed them on the table, poured her pasta from the container onto a paper plate, placed her vegetable pouch next to the plate along with crackers and goldfish, and opened up her carrot container. Tanya would also physically re-direct Emily's body, using her hands to slide Emily's leg under the table if she was sitting askew (Emily would always quickly pop her leg out again, she preferred it cock-eyed), or gently-yet-firmly wrapping her arm around Emily's belly if she wanted to stand up before she was done.

At lunchtime, Emily didn't matter; she didn't even really need to be there other than to digest the food. Her agency was effectively squashed through the infantilization of her skills and the control of her body. Adults infantilize children when they do things for them that the child can do on their own. This is a persistent pattern in the life of a young child and produces a diminished agency as the child's chance to matter, to participate, and to contribute is foreclosed. This does not occur randomly or coincidentally; this is a persistent and coordinated pattern that young children face throughout the institutions of early childhood.

This all came together one snowy afternoon in Little Ones. I had been piecing together my emerging thoughts on infantilization, musing on how adults diminished Emily's capacities by doing things for her, and it sort of hit me over the head.

Emily exited the elevator, all fluffed up with winter gear. She stood there motionless and I wrote, "Tanya is stripping down Emily – jacket, boots, socks." Like lunch, these were all things Emily could do on her own. Slower than Tanya but generally successful. Tanya knew this, confirming in a later interview, "She can put her socks and shoes on by herself, she does it." But infantilization was the normal pattern. I wrote down similar observations on other days as well:

Emily starts to take off jacket by herself. Tanya holds her right arm, finishes taking off her jacket for her, holds her arm briefly while tending to other children, then lets her go, and gives her her jacket.

Tanya takes Emily's hat and jacket, puts her hat on, puts her jacket on, Emily does none of it, then zips her jacket up all by herself.

On this day, after removing her snow gear, Tanya told Emily that her "socks are completely wet" and "I'm going to change your socks." Tanya sat Emily down on the hallway floor and peeled off her wet socks. This wasn't quite a "change," though, as there was no mention of dry socks.

It all got a little messy from here.

Emily entered the classroom, freshly barefoot, and sat down on the rug with the other students to listen to Michelle read *Froggy Gets Dressed* by Jonathan London ("Ages 3-5 years"). I peeked at the back of the book after Michelle was done; the description read: "Rambunctious Froggy hops out into the snow for a winter frolic but is called back by his mother to put on some necessary articles of clothing." The story follows a pattern in which Froggy goes out into the snow only to be called back by his mother each time because he has forgotten an item of clothing. Michelle turned aside from one page to address the Little Ones: "Do you see? Froggy has no pants. Silly froggy!"

It was eerily similar to Tanya and Emily's snow gear interactions but sort of in reverse. I jotted down in my fieldnote as I listened to the story, "Children are humorously incompetent, so we do everything for them." This seemed to sum up the Froggy story and also Tanya's interactions with Emily.

Emily stayed barefoot for the book, for lunch, and through naptime until pickup. When she woke up from her nap, Tanya was no longer in the classroom and the remaining teachers seemed to implicate Emily, not Tanya – who had actually taken Emily's socks off – for her bare feet:

Yasmin: Emily, can you find your shoes? Is this one yours?
Emily: No, Adalia's.
Yasmin: OK, so I found one of Adalia's.
Emily: These are mine.
Yasmin: But where is your sock?
Emily: I don't know.
Helen: I thought everybody was going to start putting their socks inside their shoes so that when we want to get them out, we can find them. [Helen was a fourth teacher, present only after nap time with the children who stayed until the later 6:00 pm dismissal. When she arrived, Tanya had already left.]
Yasmin: Did you find your socks?
Emily: No.
Yasmin: Oh, your socks are wet.
Emily: My socks are wet.

Emily was kind of stuck. Tanya never told her where she had put her socks, and now Yasmin and Helen were calling her out for not knowing where they were. I could picture an *Emily Gets Dressed* version of the *Froggy* book, with Michelle calling out, "Do you see? Emily has no socks. Silly Emily!" Kate entered the classroom and Emily did her best to bring her mom up to speed:

Kate: Hi!
Emily: Mom, my socks are wet -
Kate: Oh, we have other socks -
Emily: so I'm not going to wear them.
Kate: No, you are. I'll get the ones in the box.

Emily: I need my shoes.
Kate: OK we can do it.

As Kate put Emily's shoes on (something we know by now that Emily can do by herself), I jotted down, "Kate puts Emily's shoes on very rushed and rapidly, because she did not want to miss the elevator." Dry socks on, they hopped in the elevator and went home.

Silly Emily. Young children want to help take care of themselves and we don't let them. They want to communicate to adults about their lives and we don't let them.

Emily led with a true, accurate, and productive statement: "Mom, my socks are wet -" and seemed poised to explain more to Kate. But adults are always in a hurry, and always already know the solution to the problem they just became aware of, slicing off the child's chance to execute a plan or finish a story – diminishing their capacity. Emily did her best to keep going and offered another true, accurate, and productive statement, "- so I'm not going to wear them." But Kate misconstrued this as a resistance to wear *any* socks and so "corrected" her – "No, you are." But Emily *was right*, and it was self-evident – she already wasn't wearing the wet socks. She was just explaining to mom what had happened, filling her in on her past few hours.

This happens all the time – children have an experience in preschool and try, but struggle, to translate it for their parents. We have such a hard time accepting that children can fill us in about their own lives; we default to intervention and correction. Emily showed me that there is far more depth to children's statements than we typically allow ourselves to believe. We choke off the meaning in a child's statement when we fail to listen or believe the child and insist on moving forward (and usually rather quickly!). There was a whole story behind Emily's socks that Helen, Yasmin, and Kate would never find out because they couldn't see the world from Emily's perspective.

We don't see or hear children; we infantilize them.

Emily Breaks Through

Adults were always getting in the way of Emily's ideas and interrupting her Neverlands.

The adult imperialism of age-based segregation, control, and infantilization – it all left very little room for Emily to actually accomplish much, for her ideas to come to fruition, and for her agency to shine. We infantilize young children when we do things for them, treating them as incompetent and rendering them useless. We use age-based segregation to keep children away from their proximal peers and to isolate them from adult society. We control children by ordering their lives, prescribing their activities, and insisting upon the "supposed to"s of the world.

Don't get me wrong, Emily had plenty of fun and led quite a charmed life. But in terms of getting her ideas out into the world and mapping her Neverlands, adults made it hard nearly every step of the way. And that is the crucial part here – this not-mattering was grafted on to her existence simply for the sake of being two. She wanted to do things her way, to showcase her agency instead of conforming to adult expectations. Most often, this would happen in small ways as she broke through the "supposed to"s of whatever the context was. This happened frequently but you have to see the interaction through a certain frame – a rethinking of our relationships – in order to see these moments as productive or generative instead of stubborn, immature, or annoying.

In the bathroom at school while Tanya changed a friend's diaper on the changing table, Emily seized the opportunity to start a game of peekaboo with Yuval (the friend she asked for the playdate with), poking their heads out of adjacent stalls: "OK, Yuval, be in there, OK? We're gonna play peekaboo! Let's say, *peekaboo!*" She squealed as Yuval disappeared and reappeared: "Peekaboo! PEEKABOO!!" I thought this was marvelous. Tanya, not so much: "Emily – I say this every day – the bathroom is not the place to play. Please go wait in the hallway." Goodbye, peekaboo! Emily's idea – which was fun, social, interactive – was squashed.

One morning at Little Ones, Emily was enjoying gently tossing small wooden cubes on the tiled classroom floor, observing and listening as each clattered, skidded, and came to a stop. Yasmin came over: "If you want to throw something, we can throw the soft balls, these are not for throwing." Mind you, if Emily was wantonly chucking these at a friend, I would understand the request to stop. But she wasn't dangerously hurling, she was delicately exploring the blocks' physical properties. She was just curious. She was experimenting.

Outside class at dismissal time, Emily and a classmate spontaneously hugged each other, initiating a pattern in which they hugged, released, and then hugged harder (if you've spent any time with young children, you've likely seen this too). I jotted down that the hug was "getting a little bit rougher each time." I could see where this was going. "You're going to fall, both of you. Be gentle or you're going to fall down," the friend's caregiver said. They did precisely that – hug, crash, fall – eliciting a gasp from the caregiver and Kate. "Are you OK?!", Kate worried. Emily, of course, stood up and quickly squeaked, "Again, again, again!" They were exploring their bodies, becoming friends, and having fun. But it was unacceptable to her mother: "This is not a good idea!" Hugging was turned into an act of resistance, the urgent desire for a young relationship suddenly marked as disobedient.

At home one afternoon, Emily opened up the ottoman in the living room and took out Scrabble Upwords Family. The game was marked for "Ages 8+" so it already felt a bit devious – there's Emily, always reaching. Emily placed several letter tiles on the board and said, "Look at this! This is going to be a train track!" Silly Emily, that's not what they are supposed to be. "A letter train track? Do you wanna make your name?", her mom countered and pivoted her toward the intended use of the tiles. Emily gestured back to her tiles and stayed firm: "There's a big train track – I don't wanna make my name!" Adults have such a hard time letting go of the "supposed to"s, of teaching children every step of the way. What if Emily's idea was considered sufficient? Acceptable? Allowable? Kate countered again, saying "OK, I think in this game you're supposed to make words." She laid out B-O-O-K and said, "Book." The imperial adult is always reminding the child of the "supposed to" of the situation. That is the nature of the relationship: one side beseeching (demanding) the other to be more like them, at the cost of the native expressions of culture by the other side. This is a persistent trait of parents and teachers. It is so hard for us to shake: the constant, ceaseless stance of correcting the child's use of materials, modeling for them the appropriate use, and redirecting them toward the mature version of the activity. It's not the modeling that is problematic – we do this (model for our child) every time we eat, walk, and talk – it's the repetitive forcefulness that dominates the child's life and the insertion of the explicit nature of this modeling into every minute of the child's day. It is an exhausting and unnatural relationship, both for adults and children. Emily, of course, rebutted her mother's attempt to spell B-O-O-K with the tiles: "Nooo! Those are mine! I'm making a train track. These are all mine and I'm playing this."

On another morning at home, Emily was using her (actual) train tracks on the wooden floor in the dining room, all ready for school and thus granted time for playing. She carefully laid them out and John came over and crouched down next to her. They built together harmoniously until he tried to tell her how she was supposed to play – "let's change the direction" of this track piece so it would "connect this into a circle" that would have allowed the trains to chugga-chugga-choo-choo all the way around. "No!" (here we go again!). "No?" Emily picked up a bumper piece (that stops the trains from going further) and said, "We have to connect it, to right here" Dad was surprised: "We don't want to stop it, do we?" (Yes, that was exactly what Emily wanted). At this point, Emily took all the trains off the tracks, laid them on their side, and said, "So they can sleep there." Dad bought in, for a moment: "Oh, they'll sleep there, that's a good idea" (I jotted down, "with a mix of surprise and sarcasm" – again, adults tend to gently mock the child when they show up with their own idea that contradicts the adults). But he couldn't help himself, he really wanted the tracks in a circle, and so tried again: "Here, Emily, get this piece right here, and then, we can probably connect them" – "Nope!" – "If you have one more curvey piece, maybe we can connect them. Why don't you put it there?" – "That's where they sleep!" – "Can I try one thing? What about this?" (he connects the pieces and forms a full circle). Nice try, dad: "NO! NO!" Emily un-did dad's work.

Each of these thwarted moments represents extinguished Neverlands, dreams that Emily was either never allowed to fully articulate or could only express through resistance and rebuttal to adult expectations. Playing peekaboo, tumbling her blocks, rough hugs with her friend, making a train out of the board game tiles, giving her train cars a nap: we interrupt children's Neverlands so frequently and casually in the name of control, in the name of being right.

Because we are adults, and things should be done *our* way.

I also noticed little moments when Emily's indigenous culture would sneak through unadulterated, when she could articulate her Neverland and bring it to life. I walked into Emily's apartment one morning at 6:45am and Emily asked me to "shake my hair." Kate explained, "She had this plan! I asked her what she wanted to say to Noah, she said, 'Go like this!' [Kate shook her head vigorously side-to-side]. I said, 'Like, say no?' She said, 'No – shake your hair!'"

We shook our hair that day, instead of saying good morning.

There is a culture to childhood that we would do well to respect and explore rather than cast aside in our eagerness for teaching, for parenting, for development. Sometimes we ought to, simply, recognize the child in front of us for who they *are* and what they *can* do, not who they are *going* to be and what they *will be* able to do. It takes trust in your child to believe in their present-presence instead of (only) yearning for their future-mature-version.

One quiet afternoon in the apartment, Emily invited me for a game of catch: "Noah, here! Noah, here! You have to play catch." A lifelong baseball fan, this felt achievable for me! But no, my adult expectations of what we would do were ... wrong.

Noah: OK great, where should I stand?
Emily: You have to play catch right over here.
Noah: OK am I in the right spot?
Emily: Yea. This is where I can go – when I'm done you can do it.
Noah: OK you show me what to do and I'll go next.

Emily threw her ball toward me and I caught it. Wrong – I only knew about the adult version of catch. I was about to learn Emily's version:

Emily: No, that's MINE!
Noah: Oh – so what do I do, throw mine this way?
Emily: Yea.

I ask the questions of an ally throughout this scene, ceding the instructions to Emily rather than inserting my own. Note how being an ally prevents the typical "No!" that would have been there if I had taken an imperial role and explained to her how catch works. Being an ally allows her agency to be expressed without the need for resistance. There is nothing to resist – I am her ally.

Noah: OK, you ready?
Emily: I'm ready.

Emily set me up about 6 feet away from where she was standing. She held one ball and handed me a second ball. She told me to crouch, so we were at the same height. She instructed me to look her in the eyes while we each threw our own balls toward each other. As we threw, Emily called out a new instruction:

Emily: I'll get you yours.
Noah: And I'll get you yours!

After a few tweaks, and more instructions from Emily, this is the "catch" she taught me: Throw the ball, do not catch it, fetch the opposing person's ball once it has rolled to a stop, roll the ball back to its owner, and then repeat. This reminded me of Emily's requests to Kate to be on the gymnastics team, said a month apart from each other. The imperial adult would infant-ilize those statements and treat Emily like Froggy – *Silly Emily, she thinks she can be on the gymnastics team; silly Emily, that's not how you play catch.* But no, actually, her initial statements were not immature or incorrect but earnestly reflected her intention, her plan, and her vision of how things would unfold. It's just that her plan to join the gymnastics team was surprising for her mom and her instructions on how to play catch were different than what I expected.

To me, these small moments – the train tracks, the hair-shaking, the game of catch, and more like them – mattered a great deal. Wartofsky describes Emily's agency here as a "remaking of that world so that it becomes *our* world and thus involves more than simply accommodating the way the world has been made: it often involves changing it" (1983, p. 199). These little actions by Emily showed me how she used her assertiveness to create *her* version of reality, to illustrate *her* way of understanding the world, and to create the future *she* wanted rather than sit there and nod her head as adults told her about how the world works – "Here is how you play trains, here is how you say good morning, here is how you play catch." It's little stuff, but it's all she's got!

Many of the ideas that Emily had throughout the year required leaving behind the trappings of being two and engaging with the wider world – she was always trying to loosen the controlled exposure that Cannella described. Despite how difficult and infrequent it was for Emily to break out of the box of being two, it was clear that her adults knew she wanted to.

Susan was seated next to her mom at the dining room table, playing with a toy called Fashion Plates, moving pieces around to create different outfits. Emily barged in from the kitchen (where John was attempting to give her breakfast), "MOMMY I wanna sit up here 'cause I wanna see…Susan I wanna SEE!" She climbed on her mom's lap and said, "I want, that one!" She started to play the game alongside her sister. John's mother was staying with them for a couple of nights and laughed as she saw this: "Of course Emily would wanna do the grown-up thing." (*Take that, CPSC age guidelines! We need to stop making assumptions about what children like and what they are capable of.*) "I know!", giggled Kate (it's always funny for adults when children do things outside of their age expectations!). Grandma said, "Well, it says, I think, for 6 or 7 or up." I checked later and confirmed, the toy did read "6 and up." What are we supposed to do, continually remove items from children's hands, because other children of their age generally don't like them? We know children want more than the limited set of material objects we give them.

John mirrored his mother when I asked about age-related expectations during one of our evening interviews after the girls had gone to bed. He said that on a family outing to a restaurant recently, the waiter handed out drinking glasses with water to everyone except Emily got a plastic bottle: "She threw a fit! Because she wanted the fancy restaurant glass." He continued, "I think she senses it sometimes. Like, she wants the 'big kid' fork. There is something different and she wants the cool thing," to which Kate added, "the thing that everybody else has." John concluded: "I think that she sees us and Susan, and then she's like, 'I don't want this stupid kid thing.'" I loved that line and thought it captured Emily's sentiment so nicely! She was always skeptical of the controlled exposure offered to her by adults. John rattled off another example of Emily not wanting the age-appropriate item, describing that Emily prefers to use an adult chair so she can "sit on her knees to sit at the table": "she very rarely takes a highchair, but sometimes we can convince her." She wanted the real deal! But she only ever for the kid version. This happens all the time to young children and yet we insist on following age guidelines instead of listening to the actual human in front of us.

Against the odds, Emily did manage a few times that were quite thrilling for her – and for me as the witness, seeing a different vision of childhood – in which she broke through the box by escaping adult control, transgressing age-based segregation, and interacting with an older child.

Outside of her sister, there was a grand total of three times I saw Emily interact with a child who was not a two-year-old, and they were each, well, very exciting: with an older student from another class at her school, at the museum in a chance encounter, and with one of her sister's friends. I considered Stetsenko, and marveled each time this occurred as Emily was busy "creating the future in the present – affirming the future-to-come and thus *real*-izing it in the here and now." Her transgressive acts – socializing with older children – were "inventing the future, rather than merely expecting or anticipating its "automatic" arrival (Stetsenko, 2017, p. 5). She had to reach for this – it was not given to her. She created these moments by acting on her own, by going out on a limb, and by defying what adults expected her to do. By being brave.

Let's see how she did it.

Clyde was a student in the Big Ones (down the hall from Little Ones), two years older than Emily and considerably bigger. In a happy coincidence, their classes used the rooftop playground at the same time most days. I first heard about him from Emily in our Duplo interviews: "I think, make the roof right here, so Clyde can be right there. Yea, cause, so he can, and then, [she was busy arranging the rooftop playground] this is me, and he's gonna run around, to catch me! And he's gonna get me!" After this, he would come up often in our Duplo sessions, invoked by Emily as a major fixture of her preschool life. Twice while I was in Little Ones, Clyde poked his head into the classroom and found Emily. The first time, Emily said hi back and Clyde silently retreated. The second time, they met each other in the Little Ones doorway for what I recorded in my notes as "a sweet hug and kiss on the cheek."

I asked about Clyde, and Kate mentioned that Emily is "super pumped about him," and Michelle said that Emily and Clyde "gravitate towards each other, on the roof they play a lot together.... When they see each other, I think they just get like a little bit happy to see each other." Later in the year, she spoke with the Big Ones' teachers about the friendship: "We did discuss something with Daniel [a teacher in Big Ones], like, 'Oh, I think they have a connection,' just to like watch out and make sure they're playing nicely and everything." Despite the age-based segregation saturating her life, Emily had made an older friend. My mind floated back to Stetsenko: "Reality is not 'given' – rather, it is taken by persons as social actors" (p. 255) as they engage with the world in "the process of inventing the future, rather than merely expecting or anticipating its 'automatic' arrival" (p. 233). Emily and Clyde took reality and invented something new at their school – a friendship spanning a two-year age gap.

In a more fleeting moment, Emily punctured through age-based segregation while on a trip to a museum downtown with her mom and sister. We entered the museum and headed into the children's room; the sign read, "Wee Studio: Drop in. Ages: Mobile – 5 years." Kate mentioned to me as we walked in, "So they have a lot like for Susan's age – but THIS room…we're all together." Got it. Rest of the museum, for big kids; little kids stay here.

Emily didn't quite buy it.

The Wee Studio was a lovely time, despite the fact that once again Emily was mid-activity, this time painting, when the dreaded transition came: "It's time to put finishing touches on those paintings. It's almost time for music time!", called the museum educator. Time rules all. I was caught somewhat surprised by the announcement. The room had a healthy hum to it as children and adults chatted and created. I followed up afterward with the director of the studio program, who explained that the "first premise" of the class is to have "exposure to art materials" and the "second premise" is to set "clear time parameters," which meant 20 minutes of free exploration followed by music and then a read aloud – the same offering, every time, for every child. The timing was specifically for "kids that age" and was "paced to hold kids' attention" (Program Director, personal communication, August 17, 2018). Throughout early childhood, adults think very poorly of children's attention spans. We are committed to an age-appropriate pace and, very often as a result, dismiss the child's generative capacity in favor of our preference for docility. The landscape of early childhood is littered with these abandoned Neverlands, these never-painted fantasy-scapes. Emily was mid-painting but obeyed and put her paintbrush down; not so much for her neighbor, as I recorded in my fieldnotes: "One of the toddlers is growing loud and restless. Her mother calls out: 'Oh my god. I'm so sorry. She's like, she's wild, she's crazy, she's a crazy person.'"

When our guiding motivation is control, we see every deviation as wild and crazy.

Meanwhile. Emily complied, moved on to music, and we wrapped up our time in the Wee Studio. Emily knew what wonders lay beyond the space for toddlers and wanted more: "Mom, let's go upstairs!" Uh-oh. It felt a little like the beginning of a Curious George book. Kate wasn't sure – she seemed torn between letting Emily roam free and her earlier statement that she did not think the rest of the museum was appropriate for Emily. "Uh, let's see…we wanna maybe go…" Emily, as always, dug in: "Mommy! Mommy! Go upstairs! Let's go!" Emily wasn't waiting for mom. She took off while still talking: "Let's go! The stairs – and – let's GO!" As she motored herself through the crowd at the museum, I jotted down that she was "shrieking and gleeful." Like a bandit on the run, perhaps? Kate chased after her: "Hey! Slow down!" We bumped through a few crowded hallways to arrive at a wide, broad staircase covered on one side by a ramp with crag-like holds allowing a child to scamper up (rather than climb the stairs). Emily diligently climbed up, and to her surprise, was met with applause when she summited the ramp: a group of children, I guessed around ten years old, had watched her climb. They were cheering wildly for her! I wrote down, "They are delighted in her accomplishment, and she is proud as well – what a feat. This is a rare moment for her." This was a special moment as Emily, to borrow from Stetsenko again, was crafting a different future. Even young children can use their agency, in modest, mundane ways, "to always transcend both how the world positions us and its status quo" (p. 227).

Emily just never bought into the status quo. Submit or resist, I knew which Emily would choose.

On another occasion, Emily and Kate were waiting outside of Susan's school to pick her up. The walk there had been a particularly pitched argument about what Kate wanted (Emily to get in the stroller) versus what Emily wanted (to walk, of course). I'll spare you the full transcript but here is a snippet. Kate: "Do you wanna get in the stroller? And sit?" Emily: "NO NOOOO" Kate hoisted Emily up onto her hip at this point as she continued: "ahhhh hahhaaaa aahhhhhhhhahaa nooohooo. I don't want – haaaheeee nooooo NOOOO I DONNNTTTT nooooo NOOOO NOOOO IIIII EEYYYY AHHHH NOOOOO NNO NO NO NO NOO WWWWAAAAA I DON'T". Kate, always gentle even in the most difficult moments (she had been pushing the stroller with one hand while holding

Emily with the other), had calmly placed Emily in the stroller when they arrived at the school and handed her her pacifier (a rare moment of daytime pacifier use for Emily). She whispered in Emily's ear and stroked her cheek. I jotted down, "Emily is sweaty, teary, and bright red." This was perhaps the lowest point I observed for Emily; rarely was she this emotionally distraught.

But! The change was remarkable when the school door opened and dozens of eight-year-olds streamed out. Emily noticed Ruthie, one of Susan's friends, and suddenly she was exuberant. Emily hopped out of her stroller, navigated her way through a now-crowded sidewalk, walked right up to Ruthie, and started calling her name loudly. Ruthie affectionately embraced Emily and the girls held hands (Emily loved holding hands!). This reminded me of the teachers' comments about Emily's boldness during an interview a few months into the school year. I had asked what they were learning about Emily as she settled into the classroom and they grew to know more about her than just her age. Michelle noticed that "Emily was taking control" of her environment by "showing us what she does, and who she likes to play with." Yasmin described Emily's movement through the classroom: "I think she knows what she wants. I think she has a plan and I think she just is strong willed. I think she knows – I think she like has intention for what she's doing." None of this was presupposed about Emily – she was just an age when she entered Little Ones. She had to prove to her teachers – to everyone around her, constantly – that she knows what she wants, that she has intentional plans and the power to execute them.

Wartofsky adds depth to both the teachers' description and the scene happening in front of me outside of Susan's school: "the child is active in its own right, not simply imitatively, but as an agent in its own construction…in that sense of agency that concerns the initiation of actions by choice" (1983, p. 199). Emily wants this – to be with Ruthie, to be away from her mother. Children take action in accordance with their desires. Stetsenko writes that these audacious acts of agency are

often against the odds, that is, even if a particular version of what is to come in the future is not anticipated as likely and, instead, *requires struggle and active striving to achieve it*. This applies in cases when a person struggles for one's vision of "what ought to be" *in spite of the powerful forces that might be pulling in other directions*. p. 239, emphasis added

Well, here she was, taking control and acting with intention, as the teachers said, and actively striving to achieve her vision of what ought to be, as Stetsenko said. As was consistently the case, Emily had to break through the box of being two (Stetsenko's "powerful forces" pulling in other directions) to achieve these goals. This was an essentially taboo relationship – against the odds – just like Emily and Clyde who were supposed to be divided by age but found each other anyways. Emily had no business with Ruthie – she wasn't allowed to play with Ruthie and Susan once their playdate actually began (Kate to Emily: "The big kids are playing in there"), she wasn't allowed into elementary school (Emily to Susan: "You have to go to your own school – to elementary school"), camp (Kate to Emily: "You're not gonna go to camp yet"), or gymnastics (Gymnastics coach to Kate: "It's not real class!"), she wasn't even supposed to play at the same playground as Ruthie (Kate to Emily: "Susan's school doesn't play there"). Our desire to offer children a sanitized, normed childhood cuts them off from so many potential interactions and experiences. The narrow childhood we offer means children need to work very hard for these fleeting moments, these opportunities for something else.

Ruthie and Emily stood there together calmly, holding hands and waiting for Susan. Kate caught her breath and seemed to know to give Emily this space. Sometimes the sheriff can look the other way.

A few moments later, Susan exited the school building and found Ruthie and Emily. The three of them began walking toward home, Emily in between the two 8-year-olds, all holding hands. An adult was not needed here – like birds in flight, they knew the way and turned in the right direction. Emily seemed transformed, almost as if she was a different person – she was gazing up at Ruthie, star-struck. Ruthie acted motherly toward Emily, speaking in a sweet, tender voice with her. Emily stumbled slightly while walking. Ruthie placed her hand lightly on Emily's back and urged her forward, telling her gently, "Emily, let's go."

Emily, just moments earlier despondent in her stroller, found new energy. She let go of those hands, only slightly bigger than her own, and accelerated. She took off down the street about 10 feet in front of the girls at a brisk jog, forcing Kate to hurry to follow. Emily embraced her sudden freedom, and yelled out, to no one in particular: "FAST! I'M GOING FAST!!" Squealing with glee, she was completely ecstatic as she galloped ahead, faster than I had ever seen her go before.

My fieldnote now reads, "Emily is in a DELIGHTFUL mood, complete contrast to earlier."

She was moving. She was free.

References

Central Park Conservancy. (2016). Reconstruction of toll family playground. https://www.centralparknyc.org/restoration/toll-playground. Accessed March 13, 2024.

Heywood, C. (2001). *A history of childhood: Children and childhood in the West from medieval to modern times*. Polity.

Hviid, P. (2008). "Next year we are small, right?" Different times in children's development. *European Journal of Psychology of Education, 2*, 183–198.

Mountainside Medical. (n.d.). https://www.mountainside-medical.com/products/crayon-adhesive-bandages-100-count.

New York State Department of Health. (2018). *Playground safety for children ages birth to 14 years*. Retrieved from https://www.health.ny.gov/prevention/injury_prevention/children/fact_sheets/birth-14_years/playground_safety_birth-14_years.htm

Office of the Federal Register. (2019). Code of federal regulations. Retrieved from https://www.ecfr.gov/cgi-bin/text-idx?c=ecfr&tpl=/ecfrbrowse/Title16/16cfr1500_main_02.tpl

Rogoff, B. (1990). *Apprenticeship in thinking: Cognitive development in social context*. Oxford University Press.

Shalaby, C. (2017). *Troublemakers: Lessons in freedom from young children at school*. The New Press.

Stetsenko, A. (2017). *The transformative mind: Expanding Vygotsky's approach to development and teaching-learning.* Cambridge University Press.

Therell, A. (2002). Age determination guidelines: Relating children's ages to toy characteristics and play behavior (U.S. Consumer Product Safety Commission [CPSC] CPSC Staff Document).

U.S. Consumer Product Safety Commission. (2015). *Public playground safety handbook.* Retrieved from https://www.cpsc.gov/s3fs-public/325.pdf

Walmart.com. (n.d.). Retrieved from https://www.walmart.com/ip/Craft-Tape-Dispenser-with-10-Piece-Craft-Tape-Assorted/19516080

Wartofsky, M. (1983). The child's construction of the world and the world's construction of the child: From historical epistemology to historical psychology. In F. S. Kessel & A. W. Siegel (Eds.), *The child and other cultural inventions* (pp. 188–215). Praeger.

4

A New Vision for Early Childhood

After Emily

On my last visit with Emily, in February 2018, I left her a picture of the two of us to hang on her fridge and a new Duplo set to add to her collection. I text with Kate once or twice a year to check in and enjoy birthday and Halloween pictures back. It pained me a little to hear "Emily is doing worksheets" in her new classroom but I was uplifted when I heard the following year from Kate that "She's still a chatty and fiery little thing" – I joked back that "chatty and fiery" would have made a great dissertation title!

A year later, I defended my dissertation on the day of Emily's fourth birthday. She celebrated her birthday; I celebrated my defense. We were both moving on. That summer, we moved our family down to Maryland, putting our roots down as our oldest was about to begin kindergarten (age matters so much that our whole family moved because one of us was about to turn five!). I settled into a new job as the preschool director at Adas Israel Congregation in Washington, DC, six months before COVID hit. Let's do this part quickly because I still try to block it out: our school closed, the world changed, and slowly we recovered (at least, partially – the stress of that first COVID year has never really left me). Our identical twin girls were born that first COVID summer – one parent allowed in the NICU, even for two

DOI: 10.4324/9781003455929-4

babies. I put much of this work aside and changed 1000 diapers that summer (no joke).

Vaccines emerged; protocols were established; fear began to subside. Eventually, we got back into our preschool rhythm. I also realized how much I missed the classroom. It had been eight years since I left teaching to become a school director. I missed the intimacy of the relationships, the direct contact with the vibrancy of young children. I missed what had always attracted me to early childhood – the wild enthusiasm of the young child, their blurry vision of fantasy and reality, and their ceaseless production of novel ideas. And now I had my learnings from Emily to try out and work through. I didn't feel I could teach these to teachers without practicing them first myself.

I jumped back into the classroom. I co-taught our part-time two-year-old class that year, three days a week, 9:00am–1:00pm (some classrooms in our school run until 5:00pm, some until 1:00pm), while staying in the school director role as well. That was a hard year! With a nanny now at home with our infant twins, I would drop our middle child off at his four-year-old classroom, spend the morning in my two-year-old classroom, and then spend the afternoon in my office as school director. A life lived in parallel, again. I had the pleasure of a truly dynamite co-teacher, Claudia, who was smart, hard-working, and committed to a Reggio-inspired approach like me. We had a total blast together along with our gaggle of eight two-year-olds – more on this shortly. At the end of the year, I had one more class photo to place next to the others on my desk (I am not holding a squirmy child in this one!). I knew this was a one-year engagement and so it ended that June when class wrapped up – teaching while running the school was, well, difficult. Perhaps again, in a few years.

The next school year, I took on another new role, becoming an adjunct professor at the School for Jewish Education and Leadership of the American Jewish University. Teaching virtually in the evenings from my preschool office, I now had the chance to explore these ideas from yet another perspective. A child's age and developmental stage does not need to be *the only* lens through which we understand them. I built my syllabus around a non-developmental lens, encouraging my doctoral students to examine childhood through the perspective of many of the authors I have leaned on throughout this book. The course was designed to critically shift perspectives on preschool and early childhood. I was delighted to have Paula Fass (referenced in Chapter 2) as a guest lecturer in class. She reviewed historical trends in American childhood and helped expose the students to a new paradigm through which to consider preschool and childhood.

It's been quite a stretch, tugging this thread of an idea through it all. Emily grew up, but I stayed in preschool. I had more work to do.

A New Vision for Early Childhood

Carla Shalaby damningly reminds us: "There are only three institutions from which Americans are allowed no escape: prisons, mental hospitals, and schools" (2017, p. xxvii). This seemingly requisite hyper-surveillance and omnipresent control are unnecessary and uninvited. Who asked for this? Certainly not the children. And I don't think it benefits the adults much, either.

We invited Julie Lythcott-Haims into our preschool (her 2015 book was reviewed in Chapter 2) and in January 2019 she gave a presentation to a few dozen of our preschool parents. You could hear a pin drop that evening as Lythcott-Haims – a dean at Stanford University for ten years – spoke to a spellbound audience about the "encroachment of parents into the lives of college students." Lythcott-Haims' warning bell from that night has been ringing in my head ever since: "There's a cliff ahead!" Her remark is geared toward grade-school students and their parents, with the sudden independence found in college as the "cliff." She wants parents to recede from the minutiae of their children's lives well before college, so they are better prepared for the cliff of independence they face when they leave the safety of home and launch into the wide world beyond.

She worried out loud about the bewildered students she saw arriving on college campuses, each year seemingly less capable than the previous: "They've never learned how to think, do, act, cope. What if they never self-actualize?" It felt to me like she was describing Emily, not a college student. I thought about all the times that Emily's thoughts and actions were stymied by an adult response. All this encroachment, she said, gives children the hidden message that "Hey kid, you're not really capable of succeeding without me." I thought about Tanya infantilizing Emily at lunch and doing everything for her. She continued:

All of this encroachment into their lives leads to higher anxiety and undercuts their sense of self and self-efficacy. We learn these things by seeing that our actions have results, when we see the correlation between action and outcome. We are interrupting the development of their self-efficacy. We are robbing them of becoming who they are.

Exactly!

For me, this described Emily's childhood perfectly. It is so rare for young children to "see the correlation between action and outcome" because so many of their actions are met with prescribed responses about the "supposed to"s of life. It felt very reminiscent of Stetsenko's Transformative Activist Stance, which had so animated my ideas throughout my time with Emily: "The revolutionary energy of transformative agency that furnishes our world ... is the province not of the select few but of all human beings" (2019, p. 431). All humans – not only adults! – have an inner drive that seeks outcomes from their actions. But as Lythcott-Haims was reminding us, we strip children of the chance for their actions to have consequences when we put our boot down on their revolutionary energy. That can't feel great. And for the young child, it happens constantly.

Dr. Becky (by now known as the "millennial parenting whisperer" [Shafrir, 2021]), true to her 2018 email to me about "more 'trust' and less 'control'", spoke plainly on a podcast about the maladaptive impact of an over-controlling childhood and the cliff ahead:

> When our kids are young, the values that society praises in them – and in us, as their reflection – are *compliance, subservience,* and *total pliability.* You take a kid to a gymnastics class, at a place they've never been to, and the kid says "I guess I'll go with that person, I guess I'll sit..." [in contrast to a child who might waver and hesitate at the doorway] then YOU are an amazing parent.
>
> But no parent is like, "do you know what I want for my 30-year-old? I hope they blindly follow people's directions." How we interact with our kids, and how we show them what is important, that's not just gonna be released from them when they're 30.
>
> Kennedy, 2022, emphasis added

Compliance and *subservience* eliminate any expression of the child's agency, like a match being blown out. Poof. Gone, in the name of children meeting their parents' expectations. It's time for a moment of reckoning: Which do we value more for our children, their agency or their compliance?

Dr. Becky continues and illuminates the odd reversal of what we value in our children as they grow. She describes a young child who is hesitant to enter a new space – the gymnastics class, a birthday party, grandma's house – and points out that our urging them to join in anyways, despite their hesitancy, is a perversion of our values for them later in life and a breach of our trust: "What we call shyness early on we call confidence later on; what we call confidence early on, we call blindly-following-the-crowd later on" (2022). We work so hard to convince our young children to comply with every expectation, every schedule, every "supposed to" but later in life we want them to be self-aware, reflective, and true to their own experience. Imperial childhood only sets them up to tumble down the cliff. She asks us to allow our child to "gaze in before gazing out," for them to be able to consider, before entering that new space, "What do *I* want? What am *I* comfortable with?" Children need to be aware of *what they expect of themselves* before they should be compliant with the expectations of others.

This is where it gets hard, as Dr. Becky continues and describes that when adults cede ground to children (around if they should enter the gymnastics class, for example), "the answers are just going to be more inconvenient" for the parent. Parents hate being inconvenienced! We want our child to do one thing (enter the gymnastics class), and when they express a diverging behavior (not wanting to enter), we revert to control (forcing their compliance). Here's the moment of reckoning. We can challenge ourselves to trust our children, to trust that their behavior is an honest reflection of them "gazing in before gazing out." What must it feel like for the young child, after gazing in and showing their hesitancy, to have the adult insist on compliance instead? Parents and teachers should stop seeing children's stubbornness and idiosyncrasies as inconvenient and begin to see them as earnest expressions of who they are and how they relate to the world.

We can re-introduce ourselves to children and re-introduce them to the world.

What might it have looked like if instead of...

...stopping Emily's peekaboo game in the bathroom, Tanya had said to the other Little Ones, "I've noticed Emily enjoys playing peekaboo. Would anyone like to play peekaboo today?"

...following his own plan for the train tracks, John had said to Emily, "Wow, the trains are sleeping, they are not going around in circles!"

...worrying about the fierce hugs outside of Little Ones, Kate had said, "You girls are really hugging each other tightly! I can tell how much you must love each other."

...telling Emily to join the music class, Yasmin had said, "Emily, I can tell you are still hungry, I'll put out some extra cantaloupe for you and you can join music over on the rug when you are ready."

Instead of clamping down on control when children's actions confuse or confound us, we can listen to their words, their behaviors, and their emotions. We can learn to trust that they aren't being stubborn or annoying – they are just being themselves. Maybe they don't want to go into the gymnastics class, the birthday party, or grandma's house. Maybe there's something else they need in this moment. When we trust children instead of control them, when we support their agency instead of thwart it, the young child can see, to borrow Lythcott-Haims' words again, the correlation between action and outcome. The path to existing in this world on your own does not need to be like a cliff. Young children can matter, now. They can participate and they can contribute; they can be in relationships not dominated by control. We can do this.

Lythcott-Haims challenged us as parents: "What if we were treated by our family members the way we treat our children?" We would never stand for it, right? She reminded me of Tamar Schapiro (from Chapter 1): "each person is a sovereign authority whose consent is not to be bypassed…. [and yet] we do not feel bound by children's expressions of their wills in the same way that we feel bound by adults' expression of theirs." We would never treat our partners or friends the way we treat our children. To be controlling in a relationship is usually a pretty ugly thing. With children somehow, we've convinced ourselves that not only is control necessary but that it should utterly dominate the tone of the relationship. No wonder we find ourselves constantly in power struggles with young children. It's not them – it's us! We are trying to fit people into boxes and control every single aspect of their lives. We know this never works. And now we are trying it, for the first time, with lots and lots of two-year-olds.

By seeing an intimate portrait of what imperial childhood is like for the child experiencing it as well as the history behind it, my hope is that we can…

…be more sympathetic and understanding when children resist our instructions and demands.
    …see children's resistance not (only) as annoying and immature but (also) as earnest proclamations attended by committed plans to carry out their vision of the future.

...better understand the context in which this resistance occurs, and the sheer volume of adult expectations young children face each day.

...come to include children in large swaths of life rather than confine them to an age-segregated experience.

...not always be the sheriff and find a way to be an ally.

This is not simply or only about *more* control or *less* control (though that is one piece of it). It is about *moving past control* as the guiding paradigm governing our relationships with young children. There are other possibilities. This is cultural, not biological – it does not have to be this way. Our relationships with our offspring are not predetermined as predicated on control. We do this to ourselves. Which means we can undo it, also.

I wrote a Noah's Note to our preschool parents the week after Lythcott-Haims spoke, building on her remarks by taking elements of my dissertation research (I would defend three months later) to outline a new vision for early childhood:

January 2019: Touching on some of the same points as Lythcott-Haims, I look at how adults "extend control into children's lives", labeling this "adult imperialism" due to the intrusion into the sovereignty of another individual. By examining the life of a two-year-old as she begins nursery school, I offer four "stances" that a parent or teacher can take with their child or student which might mitigate the "over-parenting trap" that Julie describes and prepare our children for the "cliff" ahead:

Symmetry: Seek out moments of symmetry, rather than power, with your child. Where, when, and how do you not need to be in control? Where, when, and how can you look at them as partners, instead of less-than?

Shedding: Shed your developmental assumptions about what a child of a particular age can, or should, do. Instead, look across at the child, asking: What *can* you do? What do you *like* to do? How can I support you in doing that? The answer we find might be very different than where developmental assumptions would guide us.

Listening: Listening to a child gives them the opposite message than encroachment. When we genuinely listen to our child, the message we give is, "Hey kid, you're pretty awesome and the world needs your ideas. You belong here as a contributing member of society." The best way to do this – to listen – is quite literally to *stop talking*.

Ceding: Ceding is the most important and also the hardest. Cede territory in your child's life back to them. Where, when, and how are you present in their life in areas they do not need you? Too often we forget to "give back" areas of children's lives once we are no longer needed. Our presence becomes vestigial and anachronistic – it makes sense only because it's the only way we allow ourselves to see our child, not because they actually still need us.

Ceding territory of our child's life back to them prepares them for the cliff ahead, when – like it or not – they launch. Julie's point on Tuesday was that it is impossible to extend control into our children's lives from birth to 18 and then simply tell them, "Oh, by the way? You're on your own now."

I'd love to hear your thoughts on this – What areas of your child's life are you extending control into but want to get out of? Conversely, what areas of your child's life are you encroaching into but do not feel they are ready for you to recede from? And, in those areas, what is your exit strategy for when your child is ready for increased autonomy?

I had boiled down my lessons from Emily. I was eager to get my ideas out there and see how parents and teachers would respond. A parent in the school wrote back a few days later:

Thanks for this, Noah. I had you in mind on Monday because [my adolescent daughter] fractured her wrist and we visited many medical professionals. She and I wrote down questions together and she asked most of them. She definitely understands what happened to her wrist and how to take care of herself going forward in a more meaningful way than had I talked over her with the doctors.

It occurs to me that one reason I fail to cede territory (in addition to falling on habits) is that "doing for my kids" is part of my identity. And that's on me to change because my big kids are ready, willing, and able to assume many responsibilities in their lives.

Have you considered writing a book for a lay audience about your research? I think your ideas could change norms and practices in many communities, schools, and families!!

Thank you for the encouragement, and yes! It just took me a few years.

Back in the Classroom

I sat on this for two years while family life and COVID took over. And then, I was back in the classroom. The first two months of classroom teaching for me in the 2021–2022 school year were hard. Just plain, hard. I was a bit rusty, and so were the children – classrooms were just coming back to life after school closures and our students were all in their first group care setting. There was lots and lots of crying that fall. It reminded me of how immensely difficult the job of a preschool teacher is (*parents – the next time you see your child's preschool teacher, please, for me, give them a hug, a coffee, and a gift card to the closest burrito place; then find their school director and tell them the teachers deserve a raise*). But with love and patience, we found our way and settled in. By November, the class was grooving, and Claudia and I were having fun. Things were calm enough that I could pause, reflect, and bring my learnings from Emily into the classroom.

The day before Thanksgiving break that year, I was reading a book to the children during morning meeting, when Janie, the smallest and youngest student in the class (but not the quietest – *biological age does not dictate the capacity to contribute!*), piped up: "I have a pocket!", she squealed. Twenty-five months old, she stood up and showed us how she could smush her tiny little hand into her tiny little pants pocket. She was so enthusiastic. I was kind of annoyed. I was in the middle of a read aloud! I shushed Janie and kept reading. Re-learning how to teach – or rather, learning how to stop teaching – was not easy.

All Thanksgiving weekend I was thinking about Janie and her pockets. My thoughts went back to Emily, and I realized I had gotten it wrong: I was still teaching; I was still *controlling*. Janie had been so bold, so declarative (just like Emily), and I had been so narrow, so dismissive (just like the imperial adults in her life). Young children have real ideas that really matter. That is, until adults get in the way and mess it up. I was the sheriff and I had made Janie the outlaw. *Teaching* and *parenting* do a great job at squelching children's earnest desires and novel perspectives in the name of some far-off goal to be realized years later. But the child is alive right here, right now, right in front of my face.

This is what I learned from Emily: stop teaching. Stop parenting. Start listening. Start trusting. I had to trust that pockets were not an annoying interruption but a meaningful topic for Janie. I had to acknowledge that *Janie would influence my teaching* just as my teaching would influence Janie. Teaching is not a one-directional experience. We *both* matter in this relationship – we shape each other.

I entered the classroom Monday morning ready to stop teaching and to take Janie seriously: to acknowledge her agency, cede some control, and see where her ideas (not my ideas) could take us. Janie was young enough and new enough to school life that *she hadn't yet learned that she wasn't supposed to matter here*. She entered our classroom brimming with the audacity of human agency. In our school we write a Daily Email to parents sharing some magical moments from the day. Here is that email from Monday morning after Thanksgiving break:

November 2021: Today, pockets were a big topic of conversation!

It all started last week on Wednesday. During morning meeting, we were mid-read aloud. Janie, however, had a different agenda – her hands were busy exploring her pants pockets and as she got one hand in her pocket she suddenly exclaimed, for all to hear, "I have a pocket!" She also told us that she was looking for another pocket on the other side of her pants.

As Reggio-inspired educators, we do our best to earnestly listen to the children. Sometimes, we make sure to follow our plans as teachers but sometimes this means pivoting from our educational agenda and instead providing space in the classroom for what really matters to the children. So, in the classroom today, we asked lots of questions about pockets, wrote down in our notebooks what the children were saying about pockets, and took pictures of pockets. Here is what we learned.

Nomi had one pocket, Karlyn had a golden zipper on her pocket, and Reuben had two pockets in his sweatshirt. Karlyn then noticed that even though she had a zipper, there was actually no pocket under it! We kept exploring for pockets and the children realized that many of them have pockets on their backpacks, where they keep their water bottle. The discussion on pockets led to a few pairs of opposites, which always presents ripe learning opportunities: we talked about open and closed, inside and outside, and empty and full.

When we listen to children and give space to their ideas and energy, we realize how powerful children are – they turned something as mundane and simple as a pocket into a whole exploration and large discussion topic. We will continue to ask questions about pockets and discuss them in class. Feel free to check in with your child about their pockets at home!

Ah! This felt great to me as an educator – being able to take my research and put it into practice. *Mundane agency* – I was finally taking Stetsenko's theory directly into the classroom, now as the teacher and no longer the researcher. Vygotsky felt dangerous again, disrupting the norms of the classroom, shifting things around and supplanting the teacher's agenda with the child's yearning. And I was back doing what I loved.

But I was nervous all over again. How would the parents feel? Teachers stopping their curriculum to talk about … pockets? Because the littlest kid in the class had randomly piped up about it? Then, as before, the parents buoyed me (*pre-school teachers – parents want to hear from you! Share your thoughts. Parents believe you and believe in you. They need you and they need your insight.*). Janie's parents wrote back with this affirming message:

> Thank you for sharing this really wonderful note today. It brought us so much joy as parents – to see and feel the passion that you have for teaching, the respect that you have for your students and your willingness and eagerness to let their curiosity drive learning, and the inspiration that you draw from the kiddos. We're so grateful that our children are at a school that takes this approach to learning, and the warm environment that it fosters. And we're really proud of our Janie, of course! She was glad to report to us the number of pockets that each of her classmates had today.

Yes! Janie had even continued the conversation at home! Janie sort of dripped agency everywhere she toddled – in the classroom and at home, as she shared her ideas with those around her. She manifested the future she wanted. It reminded me of running into Zoe all those years later and hearing that her butterfly painting was now framed on her bedroom wall: her actions had outcomes that mattered. Her ideas had value in the world. Her presence was productive. She mattered.

The curriculum took off from there, and man, was it fun. For three months, a "pocket check-in" was the cornerstone of our morning meeting. The children really responded! They were so excited each morning as they arrived in the classroom to show off their pockets and check out their friends' pockets. It became part of our cultural identity and how we related to each other. The children's native culture took over the classroom and replaced our imperial agenda of what morning meeting was "supposed to" look like. We kept doing read alouds, rhyming songs, and other preschool staples, but it was all really background music. Our teaching practices took a backseat to the main event every day: pockets. Rather than teaching, we were amplifying the children's voices, helping to nurture their ideas along.

Janie was no longer the outlaw; she was a leader. Pockets became the central point of our relationship with the children. We kept the parents in the loop about our pocket check-ins through our Daily Emails:

December 1: Karlyn and Janie both found something similar – their pants look like they have pockets, but there are not actually pockets! Caleb showed us lots of pockets, on his pants and in his sweatshirt. Reuben made a big discovery – cargo pockets on his pants! They also had a flap to keep them closed.

December 6: Before we even started our Good Morning Song, Nomi mentioned – "I don't have any pockets"! But when we asked her to stand up and show her friends, we realized she DID have a pocket – up high on her shirt so she couldn't really see it! Caleb had two zipper pockets, one was open and one was closed but both were empty.

December 13: Janie was eager to share that she had a pocket on her shirt today; Simone showed how deep her pants pockets were; Karlyn found out that she had two pockets on the back of her pants; Nomi was excited to show the pockets in her sweatshirt. Caleb had cargo pockets today, and so did Reuben. Everyone's pockets were empty today – nobody found anything inside!

January 5: Janie shared her "fake out" pocket (looks like a pocket but doesn't actually open), we noticed Reuben has a picture of a fish on his shirt pocket, Ezra thought he did not have pockets but was surprised to find that he did have pants pockets, Simone showed us her pants pockets, and Karlyn and Charlie didn't have pockets but were excited to find their jacket pockets later as warm places to put their hands on the playground.

January 12: Janie and Karlyn both had "fake pockets", Ezra had the most pockets today with five and even had two cargo pockets, Reuben had two "belly pockets", Simone had two zipper pockets which she showed us how she can open and close, and Charlie had no pockets on his clothes so showed us his jacket pockets instead.

January 14: Karlyn was thrilled to have pockets today with zippers – she showed us how she can open and close them. Reuben had his famed cargo pockets, Simone had a tushy pocket, Janie her infamous "fake out" pockets, and Ezra had pants pockets – he showed us how he could put his hands inside.

January 19: Simone showed off what we decided to call "ruffle pockets" since her ruffles rimmed her pocket today. Our pocket taxonomy is expanding!

January 21: Caleb discovered that he had pockets even though he didn't think he did – we called these "surprise pockets".

Karlyn's mom wrote back at one point, and I loved her email:

This is why Karlyn has to wear real pockets and not the fake ones that most of her pants have! I had to change her pants this morning so she could have "pants with pockets". The original pants had fake pockets, but I love the excitement, so I went with it.

Janie's idea had taken root in the classroom and led to Karlyn forcing the issue with her mom, who changed Karlyn's pants because she wanted to be part of the cultural interactions that Janie had instigated. Janie proved that our trust in her idea was appropriately placed. As teachers, we were able to support the children's culture rather than supplant it with our own. Karlyn's mom became an ally instead of a sheriff, helping Karlyn choose pants with pockets instead of insisting she keep her original pair of pants on. Janie's ideas mattered not only to her, and not only in the classroom, but even to her friends and in their homes. The children were working together to establish a common culture, and we, the teachers, were their allies.

It really worked! The vision was on the ground. Here was the praxis I'd been after, bringing theory into classrooms to turn it into reality. We ceded ground by changing the morning meeting routine, listened to children by reflecting Janie's words back to her, shed our assumptions about what was supposed to happen, and found symmetrical relationships with our children.

I shared a little bit about our new pocket curriculum with the rest of the school in a Noah's Note:

> *December 2021:* Children play a meaningful role in the creation of their own community. This is a foundational precept to democracy – the citizen holds the power. Children are generally excluded from the levers of power and control throughout our culture; so, we use our classrooms to create a civic forum in which the child can stretch their muscles as citizens and see their impact on their own community. We intentionally build an environment where the children know their ideas matter.

We all want to be listened to. Young children are so rarely given the chance. We can change that by taking children's ideas seriously.

It is important to point out here that this is not about "empowering" children, which is a word often used to describe giving children power in a classroom setting. I wrote about this in a volume of collected works on educating for democracy within early childhood (Hichenberg, 2023), and the commentary following that section of the book describes my point well:

> Whereas several of us have called for educators to "empower" children's agency, Hichenberg cautions us about this framing by writing, "Power and agency here are not sought-after pedagogical goals, to instill in children through education for later use as adults within society – they are always-and-already present in the child's humanity" (this volume, p. 171). Hichenberg uses

the phrase "always-and-already" repeatedly to empha-
size that we, as pedagogues, are not empowering children; instead we are recognizing their power and agency
where it already is, by receding from a position of control.
This argument echoes Rancière (1991), who asserted that
teaching toward empowerment stultifies the student by
claiming that she lacks the power to begin with. Rather,
Hichenberg sees the child as powerful to begin with and
shows how adult imperialism attempts to hide, diminish,
or otherwise thwart that power.

   ...we wonder if it might be especially useful to frame
our advocacy for children's agency in terms of educators
"receding from control," rather than as bestowing power
upon children.

DeZutter et al., 2023, pp. 186–187

We did not empower Janie, we simply stopped preventing
her power from being felt in the classroom by receding from control. She already had the idea and enthusiasm for pockets, and
the bold audacity to share it with her classmates. That was all
her. We reflected her power back to her and gave it space to grow.
The child is *always-and-already* powerful, productive, and generative – we simply need to get out of their way and trust them
instead of correcting them.

Janie's seemingly stray comment about her pockets mattered
so much to her that we all spent months engaged with this idea. I
began to notice this around preschool more and more – these odd
ideas children have, the funny little things they do, the weird
little treasures they collect – they are whimsical but enduring,
idiosyncratic but earnest. They really do care about them. They
are the seedlings to their Neverlands, their pathways toward
the world they imagine and strive toward. And we swat them
away because we see them as trivial and immature rather than
an authentic expression of the child's native culture. We don't
understand or agree so, in our imperial relationship, we discard
them.

All that year, Claudia and I took our students on hikes in
the nearby woods. The children took to stopping at a certain

bench every time to play "ice cream": as Claudia and I waited behind the bench, they would clamber up onto it, turn around to face us, sit up on their knees, and reach their arms over the top of the bench toward us. "Do you want peach, or vanilla?" they would ask, with broad grins and twinkles in their eyes. "Do you want sprinkles?" "Five dollars!" "Eat it quick, before it melts!", they called out eagerly. It was *cute*. We smiled and played along.

The following school year, our students moved on, and I moved back into the office full time. One morning many months into the school year, a teacher's absence meant I was pulled into a class for the morning to help – a student of mine from the previous year, Caleb, was in this classroom now. They were headed out into the same woods for a hike, for the first time that year. We left school and entered the woods. And sure enough, at that same bench, Caleb climbed up, turned around, sat on his knees, and stretched his arms out toward me: "Do you want peach, or vanilla? Do you want sprinkles?" Caleb, now three years old, had kept the idea alive inside of himself this whole time – six months after our last hike, it was still very present and very real for him.

I was wrong. It wasn't *cute*, it was *powerful* – a transformation in my own perspective I continue to work on. The ice cream play was meaningful and relevant for the children, a powerful tool to coalesce their experiences and bring the group together. *They* created this, not me and Claudia. They revealed parts of their life to us; they collaborated within their peer play; they used their imagination to create something where nothing had been. Their play scheme gave them a collective identity and a social landscape in which to matter. Zoe, Emily, Janie, Caleb – my young friends have thoroughly convinced me about the power of young children's ideas, explorations, creations, and curiosity. Now I approach children's ideas and actions with reverence, knowing that much of what they express, play, or do is not a passing fancy but is actually deeply meaningful and often stretches out over many months or years. Each creative act by a child is a door opening to a new Neverland and the endless potential for expression, exploration, and meaning-making. That's not cute. That's pretty powerful.

Children Need Autonomy

To arrive at this new vision of early childhood – in which adults trust children instead of control them, in which adults and children *shape each other*, in which children's power is recognized – there are a few core concepts I keep coming back to: children need autonomy; children are complex humans; and children are not useless. These concepts chart the way for how to rethink our relationships with young children.

Edward Deci and Richard Ryan first described "self-determination theory" in the 1980s, a set of ideas on human motivation that explores the differences between intrinsic and extrinsic motivation and is used in a wide variety of settings where motivation is a key factor in accomplishing established goals, such as schools and workplaces. They explain that *autonomy* (sorely lacking in Emily's life) is one of the three elements that lead to intrinsic motivation, the other two being *competence* (being able to do the task at hand – Emily was great at this) and *relatedness* (finding relevance, meaning, or connection – again, not something Emily struggled with). These elements must work in concert, as the three inputs of autonomy, competence, and relatedness are "like a three-legged stool; pull out any one of these supports and the stool will fall" (2017, p. 250). In his brilliant book, *Why We Do What We Do: Understanding Self-Motivation* (1996), Deci writes that

> Controlling people – that is, pressuring them to behave in particular ways – diminishes their feelings of self-determination. An overemphasis on control and discipline seems to be off the mark. It represents a demeaning depiction of human experience, and its primary function may just be to *provide certain people with an easy rationalization for exerting power over others*. pp. 33–34, emphasis added

This was precisely what was occurring in Emily's life. Recall Michelle's line, "We technically do whatever we want, right? They are in our control, right?" Emily was constantly pressured to behave in particular ways as others exerted power over her. Deci and Ryan's theory provides insight into the impacts this may have, into the "so what" of it all. They explain that autonomy (as well as competency and relatedness) is an essential human need that is foundational in the pursuit of "ongoing psychological growth, integrity, and well-being" and that it "plays a necessary part in optimal development" and "psychological health" (2000, p. 229). They write with urgency that autonomy cannot "be thwarted or neglected without significant negative consequences" (p. 229) – *this is precisely what happens to young children.*

The pair spent decades conducting dozens of research experiments with students, young and old, around the effects of different types of motivating inputs. Deci reports the result of one such study which explored the impact of two types of instructions to five- and six-year-olds around the task of painting a picture: one group of students had "conventional, controlling" instructions ("Do as you should and don't mix up the colors") and the other had "noncontrolling, autonomy-supportive" instructions ("I know that sometimes it's really fun to just slop the paint around, but here the materials and room need to be kept nice for the other children who will use them.") He reports that

> the results were dramatic … the autonomy-supportive condition seemed to have a liberating effect on the children, while the controlling condition had a debilitating effect. The children who sensed that *the adults at least understood them* were more intrinsically motivated and more enthusiastic than the children for whom the limits had been more controlling.
>
> 1996, p. 43, emphasis added

Adults can shift their focus away from control and toward understanding while still providing clear structure. Cutting back on control is not a devolution into anarchy, it is an invitation for psychologically sturdier children. And for adults, it is an invitation for a more sensitive, engaged, resonant, and attuned relationship with the child, an overall more caring and respectful parenting and teaching. Trust is good for both partners in the relationship.

I have long shared with preschool parents an interview with Jeree Pawl, clinical psychologist specializing in the mental health of young children for over 50 years, where she touches on how overparenting interferes with a child's developing sense of self (which is nothing but a central task of childhood!). Pawl advises that when young children are presented with obstacles (navigating around a crowded room, conflict resolution with a peer, being bored while waiting in line, etc.), adults would be wise to

> give them the message that there are things *they can do*: "You can entertain yourself, you can sing to yourself, you can do all kinds of things so that you don't, in that moment, *need that other person* [a parent or teacher]. You will find your way through it." The more parents intervene, the more they try to persuade, the worse it is.
>
> 2012, p. 25, emphasis added

Like Lythcott-Haims for older children, Pawl's point is that for young children to develop a strong sense of self-esteem and self-efficacy, they need to be able to see that their actions have outcomes – that they can do things, too, not only their adults.

This is a concept picked up by the Let Grow project, co-founded by Jonathan Haidt and Lenore Skenazy in 2017 along with Peter Gray and Daniel Shuchman (Haidt, 2024, pp. 254–256), in which children (kindergarten through middle school) are encouraged to "go home and do something you've never done on your own before. Walk the dog. Make a meal. Run an errand" (p. 254). Haidt argues that parents have been frightened into "over-supervising their children" (p. 240) and that, resonant with my argument here, "when we give trust to kids, they soar. Trusting our kids to start venturing out into the world may be the most transformative thing adults can do" (p. 256). Trusting children and ceding their independence back to them offers them a radically altered relationship with themselves and the world.

Haidt describes a 7th grader in the Let Grow project who got her five-year-old sister ready for school and helped her board the school bus who reported that when the bus pulled away, "I felt really important to her, important to someone." Haidt succinctly describes the transformative impact on the 7th grader: "At last, instead of feeling needy, she was needed" (p. 256). Imagine a preschooler being able to access that feeling too.

Camilo Ortiz and Lenore Skenazy (clinical psychologist and board member at Let Grow) explore what children can do by themselves despite the highly regulated nature of contemporary childhood:

> Parents … now believe that the more supervised, structured activities they can put their kids in, the better off they will be. We think this constant supervision and intervention could be hurting kids' chances to become brave and resilient. What's missing today isn't just the thrill of climbing trees or playing flashlight tag. It's that when an adult is always present – in person or electronically – kids never really get to see what they're made of.
>
> What if the problem was simply that kids are growing up so overprotected that they're scared of the world? If so, the solution would be simple, too: Start letting them do more things on their own. This is exactly what the two of us have been studying.
>
> 2023

Not surprisingly, they find that "teachers and parents have told us that kids' confidence starts climbing" when they begin to do new things on their own that they had previously only done with the supervision or assistance of an adult. Accordingly, Haidt urges parents and teachers in *Anxious Generation* to "reduce rules and increase trust" (2024, p. 261) and that we "need to start prevention early, in elementary and middle schools, *before* our children begin wilting" (p. 263). In this sense, this and the following chapter can be considered as ways to extend this train of thought even earlier, into the overcontrolled, imperial childhood of the preschool years. The drive toward independence and self-actualization is ongoing; it does not begin in kindergarten.

Young children need to know they can do things without adults. And the ever-present adult, simply and bluntly, robs them of this. The adult trying harder, or trying new strategies, is not effective here – the parent or teacher has to literally remove themselves, cede the ground to the child, so they can work through it on their own:

> "I'm so sorry your *fill in the blank* fell apart. I need to finish washing the dishes. I know you can fix this without me." (Don't fix it for them!)
>
> "Eek! You're under the table and not sure how to get out! Use all your muscles and see what you can do, I believe in you!" (Don't move the chairs for them!)
>
> "Ouch, I noticed that friend pushed you on the playground while waiting turns for the slide. I know you're having so much fun playing though. Get back out there and I'm sure you can figure out a way to solve this." (Don't approach the peer!)
>
> "Oh no, your block bridge keeps falling down. I wonder if there are other ways you can try to build it. Have you asked any friends for help?" (Don't build the bridge for them!)

Madeline Levine, psychologist, clinician, and author, addresses the question "Does overparenting hurt, or help?" in an article that I've likewise shared with many preschool parents and teachers over the years. She describes how "psychological control" over our young children brings with it "damage to a child's developing identity":

> The happiest, most successful children have parents who do not do for them what they are capable of doing, or almost capable of doing; and their parents do not do things for them that satisfy their own needs rather than the needs of the child.
>
> The central task of growing up is to develop a sense of self that is autonomous, confident and generally in accord with reality. If you treat your walking toddler as if she can't walk, you diminish her confidence and

distort reality. Ditto nightly "reviews" of homework, repetitive phone calls to "just check if you're O.K." and "editing" (read: writing) your child's college application essay.

Once your child is capable of doing something, congratulate yourself on a job well done and move on. Continued, unnecessary intervention makes your child feel bad about himself (if he's young) or angry at you (if he's a teenager).

2012

She concludes by describing how "If pushing, direction, motivation and reward always come from the outside, the child never has the opportunity to craft an inside." That's exactly it – all these years, I've watched as children are essentially bossed around by their adults, with everything about their life coming from the outside – from their adults – and almost none of it coming from the inside – from themselves.

We need to cede ground and give an internal locus of control back to our children.

Emily's ideas were constantly thwarted by adults as external expectations superseded her internal thoughts. This is so common in early childhood that we rarely step back and wonder what it would be like for children to have greater autonomy. We believe children need to be controlled, and so we control them. Any maladaptive results we then attempt to smother with behavioral strategies and more control. It's not working: the stool is collapsing and there is a cliff ahead.

Young children need greater freedom and more autonomy. *Humans* need autonomy, not only adults.

Children Are Complex Humans

Humans are complex. Just look at you or me. We don't fit well in narrowly defined boxes. We are more than one thing. We are not the color of our skin, our country of origin, and certainly not our age. Those things are a part of us, but they are not *who we are*.

If we are to move on from an imperial childhood, we need to be able to look at children through this same lens: they are humans, not only an age.

There is no monolithic childhood. This idea that all children of the same age need the same thing, at the same time – what we might call a panchildhood – *exists only in textbooks and policies*. It is not an accurate portrayal of real children, doing the real work of childhood. The gap between these – between the theory and the real world – poses a heavy burden on parents, teachers, and children, as we attempt to reconcile the gulf between the imagined, normed child and the messy human in front of you. The whole idea sets everyone involved up for stress, anxiety, and failure – we are pining after something that just does not exist. Our goals are misguided.

To be a child is not to be something static, something simple, or something easily describable. My preschool hosts 120 children each day. None of them are the same – the *only* quality that unites them is their biological age. That single factor should not be used to create a flat space of childhood for them. Some run into school; some walk gingerly behind their parent's leg. Some are loud and verbal; some are mute and bashful. Some warm to new teachers instantly; others take many, many months. Some learn quickly; some learn slowly. Some know how to share, some do not. Some are described as neurotypical, some as neurodiverse. At their own pace, in their own way – they all need to find a space in preschool that recognizes them for who they are, not for their distance from the imagined, fictional behavior of a "normal" child.

Like you or I, children have distinct personalities and identities, backgrounds and values, countries of origin and kinship structures. Being two is a *part* of who a child is but, as a complex human, it does not define their existence. The same can be applied, of course, to the ideas in this book – perhaps *some* children will benefit from more autonomy and greater freedom, while *others* may find it frightening and anxiety-provoking to not have clear guidance. There is no formula, there is no scripted guidance, *there is only diving into the relationship and trusting the person you find.*

Early childhood education and developmentally appropriate practices don't quite provide the proper lens through which to do this. Instead, they leave us with grand narratives about a broad class of people, sidestepping the variation that occurs among individual children as well as the historically changing nature of childhood (think about what Emily's life would have been like in 1875 – today's "developmentally appropriate practices" would not have been ... appropriate). As a result, an "essential" child is created – a single, unified image of a child that is stable, innate, and unchanging, which we expect all children to fit into. They should all walk into school nicely, say hello courteously, and settle in smoothly, following instructions and schedules along the way. We are then anxious when our child does not fit into that mold of the essential child (none of them do!), and so we clamp down on control to push them back into that single-framed expectation. It's a bad recipe.

The idea of fixed development and a normed childhood led American parents and teachers to believe that all children always go through the same stages. *This is not true.* Rogoff illuminates how even something like the "terrible twos" is a cultural construction and not a biological reality rooted in the age of the child:

> In middle-class European American communities, the end of infancy is expected to involve a sudden appearance of contrary behavior – the "terrible twos" ... categorized as being obstinate, negative, and needing independence.
>
> In contrast, in many communities, such a transition to negativism and obstinacy around age 2 is not observed or expected.... For example, Zinacantecan infants in Mexico do not go through this transition; instead, they are watchful and observant, seeking contact with mothers who until then had treated them with a special status now reserved for a new baby.... Rather than asserting control and independence from their mother, they change their status from mother's baby to a child of the courtyard children's group – a child who

acts as a responsible caregiver to the new baby and helps with household tasks.

2003, pp. 167–168

Canella offers a similar stance on the wild variation within what two-year-olds can do:

There is no particular way that a 2-year-old will act. In some cultures s/he may be skillfully cutting fruit or reproducing communication dances. In others, s/he may be assisting in caring for babies. In still others, s/he may be exerting independence by saying "no."

1997, p. 150

Despite current mainstream views on young children in America, children of the same specific age share *very few* inborn biological qualities. Modern society has moved past outdated grand narratives of what social groups and labels are *supposed to be like*, such as "All women are…" or "All immigrants are…." But that view still holds sway about children. We use age in formulaic fashion all the time with young children when we say things like, "C'mon, you're a big kid now, you can do this!" or "You're not a little kid anymore, don't do that." "Being a child" is a cultural status and a social category, not only a biological stage. We can challenge the notion that being a child means the same thing for each person the label is applied to and that all children have similar needs and competencies. This just isn't true. Instead, perhaps, we can recognize children – as humans – for what they can do in terms of *competency* instead of in relation to their labeled social category of age.

Consider a few ways in which Emily's competencies were referred to under the sweeping generalization of her age: Tanya said, "her language is very sophisticated *for her age*" and "no matter how mature she acts – she is *still a toddler*," the grandpa at the playground remarked "You are very chatty *for just a two-year-old*," and Kate reminded herself, "oh right – *she's two*." Try replacing "age," "toddler," or "two-year-old" in those sentences with other social labels (woman, immigrant, poor, queer, etc.). Say them out loud. Are you comfortable with it? Would you say that to an adult? Here is a way to rethink the language we use in our relationships with young children around competency and age:

> "You're really struggling with the potty, and I'm here to help you" replaces "You're a big kid, you need to be able to do this."
>
> "That's so cool, you love snapping your fingers" replaces "Whoa, I didn't know three-year-olds could snap!"
>
> "Do you think you'll like that puzzle?" replaces "That puzzle is too hard for four-year-olds, let's try a different one."

Our singular focus on age as the defining feature of children assumes that all two-year-olds have the same interests (Daniel Tiger), have the same attention span (short), and are easily swayed by treats (lollipops). This ignores how other parts of the child's identity intersect with their age – such as their individual interests and tastes and their varying cultural contexts. Each child, like each human, has a unique cultural fingerprint. They do not fit neatly or squarely into any one box or social category. They are not replicas of their parents nor mirrors of their peers – they are only themselves. There is infinite variety across children, a distinctiveness to each child, a uniqueness to each of their possibilities.

We need to stop flattening children, and childhood, by insisting on a one-size-fits-all model. We can do this by withdrawing from our insistence on seeing children as an age and instead seeing them as humans with complex, varying, and divergent needs, wants, and personalities.

Children Are Not Useless

Young children are not actually useless. I promise you.

It's that we've trained them to be useless and trained ourselves to expect nothing from them. All over the world, all throughout human history, young children have actively contributed to the family, or household, or whichever kinship structure and cultural context they were born into. The sanitized, useless childhood created in twenty-first-century America robs children of the chance to matter by creating childhood as a space which is barred from contributing or participating in any meaningful capacity. Think about Emily at lunch, or getting her haircut, or trying to make a playdate. The childhood presented to her did not *allow* her to contribute to, or participate in, those activities. She was stripped of her agency and *made* to be passive.

Mattering, in this sense, is not only about seeing one's ideas impact the world (thought that is a part of it). It is also about mattering to those around you through collaborative work and helpful contributions. I matter because I help; I matter because I do things. I have a role and my work is valued here. These messages are all absent from the young child's life as they encounter hyper-controlling adults who eliminate their opportunity to participate in activities such as cooking, cleaning, household chores, and cultural activities.

Anthropological literature is full of ways that children matter, in the sense of participating and contributing, around the world and throughout history. It is this specific time and place that has *created* the useless child. Rogoff maintains that "in many other communities around the world, children begin to take on responsibility for tending other children at ages 5-7" (2003, p. 4) such as a six-year-old Mayan girl in Guatemala who is a "skilled caregiver for her baby cousin" (p. 5). She also shows how safety is relative and needn't prevent children from using authentic tools to help out around their community:

among the Efe of the Democratic Republic of Congo, infants routinely use machetes safely...Fore (New Guinea) infants handle knives and fire safely by the time they are able to walk...Aka parents of Central Africa teach 8- to 10-month-old infants how to throw small spears and use mall pointed digging sticks and miniature axes with sharp metal blades. p. 5

I had this in mind while observing in a preschool classroom for morning meeting. Celebrating Asian American and

Pacific Islander Heritage Month in May of 2024, the class was reflecting on a book they had recently read together, *Cora Cooks Pancit* (Gilmore, 2014). The book shows how Cora, a young girl, cooks *pancit*, a Filipino noodle dish, with her mother. Cora even does the "grown-up tasks" like shredding the chicken and soaking the noodles. One four-year-old student was dubious and spoke up: "How could a little girl cook soup? She's not big, like a grown up." I imagined the preschooler in conversation with Rogoff, who might have responded, "Mayan children in the Guatemalan town I have worked in began to make a real contribution to household work by age 4 to 6 years – tending infants, delivering messages and running errands around town, and helping with meals and agricultural work" (p. 168). The distinctions between what a child can and cannot do are largely cultural, not biological.

It's not that children *can't* participate in mature community activities like cooking, it's that we don't let them. It's us, not them! And I don't think we actually want our children to be useless, it's that we've been led to believe there is no other way. But there is. It's simple and radical: children can do things. Real things. With real tools. They don't need to live secluded in the box of early childhood, stuffed into preschool classrooms and showered with age-graded toys, cut off from the actual happenings of the world. Their world can be broader. There is an excellent model for how to frame this – children's participation in doing real things – called *legitimate peripheral participation* (Lave and Wenger, 1991). The idea is profound yet basic: beginning as novices, humans learn to do the things they participate in peripherally, until they become masters. The key piece here is that skills and competencies are products of *participation*, not of *age*. Cora learns to cook because her family *involves her in cooking*, not because Filipino children have markedly different biological capacities than American children. Lave (2012) maintains, "We are always learning what we are already doing"– *doing things* is how humans learn the technical skills and craftsmanship which allow them to fully participate in their cultural context. Lave is a social anthropologist and, like Rogoff and her ideas about apprenticeship, her work on learning rests on Vygotsky's school of sociocultural thought. Vygotsky's ideas can be made dangerous again by discarding the notion that children are useless and showing us that *children can do real things*. This completely upends how we view what children can do and what they need from their relationship with adults – in my view, it upends the whole field of early childhood. Children need to *do*, not *prepare*. They need to *participate in real life* rather than be *instructed about it while removed from it*.

Consider the cornerstone of developmentally appropriate practices, reviewed in Chapter 2: "we first think about what children are like within a general age range" such as "the number of [puzzle] pieces 4-year-olds typically find doable" (Kostelnik et al., 2011, p. 20). Legitimate peripheral participation would take a radically different formula and insist that children who have tagged along with more accomplished others (siblings, neighbors, parents, etc.) while they did puzzles and helped with peripheral tasks such as flipping the pieces over, or finding the pieces with straight edges, or even just picking up pieces that might have fallen to the floor would be able to accomplish puzzles of a far greater complexity than "typical" four-year-olds. And your first reaction reading that is that young children don't have the patience, focus, or complexity of thought for those tasks – they would throw the pieces or draw on them or try to eat them. That is only true about children who *haven't been legitimate peripheral participants* of those actions. But a child coming from a family that does puzzles together, exposed to the practice from a young age, would find a four-year-old puzzle in their preschool classroom to be laughably simple.

The question of what is "appropriate" in this re-oriented relationship with children shifts to revolve around not how old the child is but what *participatory experiences* the child has. Reformulated as such, developmentally appropriate practices, as they stand, can be seen as diminishing the child's capacity by preventing them from participating in large swaths of life. Our modern reverence for the child's age is a distraction and an ill-advised gatekeeper. Young children can do real things when they participate in them. When they participate in nothing, they learn that they are useless.

References

Deci, E. (1996). *Why we do what we do: Understanding self-motivation.* Penguin Books.

Deci, E. L., & Ryan, M. R. (2000). The "what" and "why" of goal pursuits: Human needs and the self-determination of behavior. *Psychological Inquiry, 11*(4), 227–268.

DeZutter, S. L., Coleman, J., Hichenberg, N., Menezes, I., Neilson, A., Rios, C., Sunal, C. S., & Whitford, A. (2023). Collaborative commentary: How do children think about and enact citizenship? In S. L. DeZutter (Ed.), *International perspectives on educating for democracy in early childhood: Recognizing young children as citizens* (pp. 185–188). Routledge.

Gilmore, D. L. (2014). *Cora cooks pancit* (Standard edition). Lee & Low Books.

Haidt, J. (2024). *The anxious generation: How the great rewiring of childhood is causing an epidemic of mental illness.* Penguin Press.

Hichenberg, N. (2023). "I don't want you to say no, I want you to say yes": One two-year-old's transformative dissent. In S. L. DeZutter (Ed.), *International perspectives on educating for democracy in early childhood: Recognizing young children as citizens* (pp. 167–184). Routledge.

Kennedy, R. (2022). *We can do hard things* (podcast), *#130: Breaking cycles & reparenting yourself with Dr. Becky Kennedy.* https://podcasts. apple.com/us/podcast/we-can-do-hard-things/id1564530722?i= 1000579281486

Kostelnik, M. J., Soderman, A. K., & Whiren, A. P. (2011). *Developmentally appropriate curriculum: Best practices in early childhood education.* Pearson.

Lave, J. (2012). *UC Berkeley Graduate Council lectures,* March 2012. https:// www.youtube.com/watch?v=FAYs46icCFs&t=33s, accessed June 17, 2024.

Lave, J., & Wenger, E. (1991). *Situated Learning: Legitimate peripheral participation.* Cambridge University Press.

Levine, M. (2012, August 4). Raising successful children. *New York Times.* https://www.nytimes.com/2012/08/05/opinion/sunday/raising-successful-children.html

Lewis, K. Abandon parenting, and just be a parent. *The Atlantic*, 2016. https://www.theatlantic.com/family/archive/2016/09/abandon-parenting-and-just-be-a-parent/501236/

Ortiz, C., & Skenazy, L. This simple fix could help anxious kids. *The New York Times*, September 4, 2023. https://www.nytimes.com/2023/09/04/opinion/anxiety-depression-teens.html?smid=nytcore-ios-share&referringSource=articleShare&sgrp=c-cb

Pawl, J. (2012) Developing self-esteem in the early years. *Zero to Three*, January 2012, 22–25.

Ryan, R. M., & Deci, E. L. (2017). *Self-determination theory: Basic psychological needs in motivation, development, and wellness.* Guilford Press.

Shafrir, D. (2021, June 26). How Dr. Becky became the millennial parenting whisperer. *Time Magazine.* https://time.com/6075434/dr-becky-millennial-parenting/

5

Stop Teaching, Stop Parenting

Stop Teaching, Stop Parenting

The ideas outlined in this chapter offer ways in which adults can stop teaching and stop parenting in order to recede from a position of control and instead:

Do less: give children the time and space needed to express their thoughts and complete their plans without turning into an outlaw, and,

Involve more: provide an entryway for children to participate meaningfully in the wide world instead of being cut off and kept within the narrow box of early childhood.

I learned from Emily that this really doesn't take much – we just need to stop. We need to stop parenting and stop teaching, leaving more space for children to fill.

Young children do not need the stimulation of a teacher, a curriculum, or suggested activities by parents *to have ideas* and *to do things*. There are no special skills that teachers or parents need here other than a little patience (OK, fine, a lot of patience) and some self-awareness in the moment. Besides that, it's just peeling back, listening, and giving the child's ideas and competencies more room to flourish. This is hard, but it is simple.

DOI: 10.4324/9781003455929-5

Alison Gopnik, psychology professor and influential author, hits the nail on the head in her 2016 book, *The Gardener and the Carpenter: What the New Science of Child Development Tells Us About the Relationship Between Parents and Children* (read this book!):

'Parent' is not actually a verb. To be a wife is not to engage in 'wifing,' to be a friend is not to 'friend,' and we don't 'child' our mothers and fathers. To be a parent—to care for a child—is to be part of a profound and unique human relationship, to engage in a particular kind of love. The purpose of love is not to change the people we love, but to give them what they need to thrive.

Gopnik expands on this theme in an interview with *The Atlantic* (brilliantly titled, "Abandon Parenting, and Just Be a Parent"): the adoption of "parenting" as a verb (which took place a short 50–60 years ago), and the cultural ramifications on both parents and children, has been

a terrible invention. It hasn't improved the lives of children and parents, and in some ways it's arguably made them worse. For middle-class parents, trying to shape their children into worthy adults becomes the source of endless anxiety and guilt coupled with frustration. And for their children, parenting leads to an oppressive cloud of hovering expectations.

Lewis, 2016

There are times that we can – and should – simply *stop*. We don't have to keep parenting or teaching until things are done exactly as we want them. Children will grow up, learn to give a proper greeting, to clean up after themselves, to stay at the table during meals, to wait their turn for the playground slide. But they won't learn it all, right now, just because a parent or teacher keeps reminding them how to do it. Children do not need adults involved in the small, repetitive details of their life. Micromanaging their life is not helping them, or us. Adult anxiety, hovering, and control are not only not helping children, but it is actively holding them back. They don't need reminders about the precise specifics of how to do ... everything. Our insistent omnipresence in the minutia of their lives does not make us better parents or teachers nor does it help them learn or grow any faster. But that is exactly what adult relationships with young children have become – endless involvement in *everything* the child does.

This is really hard – knowing when to let go and stop parenting. Remember that there is no always-right answer. This is about your relationship with your child, not about following the prescriptions of others. Think about it like picking your battles. Consider ten interactions with your child in which they protest your expectations, like Emily. How about in one of those interactions you just stop? Yield. Cede. Relent. You fought the last nine battles. Can you become an ally this time?

Keep in mind, this is not an invitation for anarchy. Firm rules and clear boundaries, for the things that matter most to you, are important for a child to internalize. Nor is this an invitation for neglect. Children obviously benefit from the presence of strong adult role models and need lots of adult love in their life. They just don't need *constant rules* and *endless supervision*.

In this new vision of early childhood, we can seek out moments of *symmetry rather than power*. We can *shed our developmental assumptions* about what a child is capable of. We can *listen to children* instead of always giving instructions and "supposed to"s. We can *cede territory back to children*. We can rethink our relationships with young children away from control and toward trust.

Do Less

Unsupervised children no longer exist. This is a symptom of our anxieties – a total and complete supervision of everything (everything!) that happens in a young child's life – and it is not necessary or helpful. Young children do not need constant supervision despite our fears and anxieties – those are *our* issues to work through, not our child's. It's burning us out. It's driving us crazy – needing to constantly be there, in control, as a parent or teacher. It's just not needed.

At a local playground for a school-wide playdate (a hundred kids running around is kind of my happy place, what can I say!), I was chatting with a mother new to the school. Or, trying to. As if she was her child's shadow, the mother urgently followed the herky-jerky movements of her 18-month-old daughter as she toddled around, with mom lurching after the child's each movement to stay close to her. Mom's arms were slightly raised and outstretched, as if poised to rescue her daughter should she fall or bump into something. This is a common stance for parents of young children – we must protect them or else they will shatter (contrast this with an Efe child of the same age, deftly wielding a machete!). None of us wake up craving this state of constant supervision but it is pushed toward us by the historical, social, and cultural forces outlined in Chapter 2: we are having fewer children later in life, leaving us seeing each single child as more precious and therefore needing to be more carefully safeguarded; we are taught they are fragile and incapable of succeeding without heavy adult intervention and instruction; we are told we are to blame for their every stumble and failure. So we never let go. We have this one precious treasure that took us three decades to arrive at – and, damn it, we will protect it at all costs. Everything I've worked for – family, happiness, continuity – could evaporate instantly, because I wasn't actively parenting. My child will fall, they will be permanently damaged, their life course will be changed, and I will never be the parent I worked so hard to be.

We need to escape this paradigm. We need to *do less*.

I caught mom's eye as she was crouched over her toddler. I lifted my hands up slightly, showing both palms, and pushed them down gently twice, the message being to pump the breaks, slow down, and back off a little. This is a well-practiced move for me: I find myself often needing to remind parents to give their child (and themselves!) some breathing room. The mother let out a sigh, relaxed her body frame a bit, and stood next to me as we watched her child explore. The child got about 15 feet away from us and mom mentioned to me with a mix of delirium and relief, "This is the farthest she has ever been from me at a playground!" Her husband came over to join us and asked what we were chatting about, and the mother was quick to say, with a smile, "Noah was suggesting I stop being a helicopter parent!" The three of us stood there for a moment enjoying the sight as their child moved on her own volition without a hovering adult-helicopter. However briefly, she was free (the child, and the mother!).

Parents can lean on each other for this – in a world full of competitive hyper-parenting, perhaps we can strike a balance by encouraging each other to chill out a little. To back off.

During any given week, how much time is your child unsupervised? Check-in with other parents on this question as well – in my experience, the most common answer is "zero", often accompanied with a skeptical look. Whatever your answer is, try to stretch it. Consider Hannah Rosin's reflection while reporting on childhood independence and resiliency: "When my daughter was about 10, my husband suddenly realized that in her whole life, she had probably not spent more than 10 minutes unsupervised by an adult. Not 10 minutes in 10 years (*The Atlantic*, 2014)." Try to beat that! It's a low bar and I believe our children, and we as parents, will benefit from a few more minutes here and there throughout the week in which we are not busy supervising and parenting.

Your child can exist without you – they can thrive without you – for batches of time. At home, when your young child has settled into a groove – playing with their toys, looking out the window, enjoying a snack – you can leave the room. You do not need to be there hovering as she plays, inevitably offering instruction and reminders about the "supposed to"s of her toys. She needs some space from you, and you from her. If leaving the room is too much, try simply letting your child know that you'll get to them "next": "Honey, I heard you, and I will come play next. I can only do one thing at a time and right now I am folding the laundry/talking to a friend/fill-in-the-blank."

At the playground, once your child gets their motor going (which for some is right away and for others only after a half-hour of clutching your legs), give them a wave and a smile: "I'll be over here on the bench if you need anything. Have fun!" Sit down with a book. *Turn away from your child.* Try this for 30 seconds. If you've never done it, it will feel like a lifetime, and you will be certain your child has fallen into peril. Look up and find them – there they are, running with glee. They are sturdy. Try it again for 60 seconds. Prove to yourself that your child does not need constant supervision and, significantly, that you can do things other than supervise your child.

One way to do less and stop parenting is a sleepover. Parents are actual humans who, when their child is not present, have the fleeting chance to shed their parenting hat. The sleepover – yes, not the sleep-under, even for a very young child – is a remarkable opportunity to remind ourselves that our child does not need our constant presence and that we do not need to be constantly parenting. Our child can thrive, even at bedtime and those groggy, intimate middle-of-the-night moments, under the care of a friend or neighbor. You're likely thinking, *"But my little one is not ready yet for a sleepover!"* Allow me to be the one to let you know, with gentle kindness: she is ready. And after one thousand consecutive nights of caring for her, you likely need a night without her, a night where you can not only do less but do nothing at all.

Horizontal Parenting

Noah's Note, March 2019: Paula Fass writes, "Today's parents are much more often seen as hovering than hands-off, and their faults lie in excessive supervision, not the reverse." Beyond making parents (and mothers in particular) overwhelmed with stress, there's a buried secret here: children do not need us in their lives nearly as frequently as we think (or hope). This is not only true for middle and high schoolers, but our young ones as well. (Yes, even our crawlers!!)

KJ Dell'Antonia recognizes this in her book published this summer, "How to be a Happier Parent": "We expect our constant attendance itself to be enough to get the job done. We show up relentlessly, as though looking for a good attendance award, when we might teach our children more by being less present."

I so loved that line. It gave me permission, and I hope you as well, *to be less present*. To accept that you are already present – and worthy – enough. That your unconditional love is the ingredient your child needs, not your unconditional presence. That they need to carry your love around with them; they don't need to carry YOU around with them.

Talking this idea through with a friend recently, a parent to a newborn and a toddler, she nodded her head and smiled: "Yea yea yea, that's what I call 'horizontal parenting'." Intrigued, I asked what she meant. "Here's how it goes: I lie down on the couch, horizontal. You play on the rug with your toys. We stay out of each other's way. That's the whole thing."

Horizontal parenting! I loved it. Robyn Isman, my lifelong friend, wasn't being flippant, she was just being colloquial – she is a clinical social worker providing therapy and support for parents of young children, focusing on how to reduce anxiety and stress in the relationship. Your child does not always need you. You can stay on the couch. I picked up the theme again after moving to Washington, DC:

Noah's Note, March 2023: OK, listen up people! If you're a parent – and you are – we need to talk about something. We give our children too much attention. We do too much for them. We step in, we help out, we pave the way…we are always there, doing something for them.

Can't we just let kids…be kids? Need we be so present?

Give your child the gift of time without you next to them so they can experience boredom, solitude, and the joy of self-discovery.

A preschool parent reached out months later, sending me a text message after intentionally leaving the area in the house where her young children were playing:

> 'Being less present' has led to 75 minutes of entirely self-directed and deeply imaginative play. Last I heard, they were pirates building ships and burying treasure. My house is a complete wreck (*she included a picture of her children amidst a pile of what looked like laundry, beads, and assorted "treasures" of childhood*) but my children – my children are loving their life right now.

Horizontal parenting, or *taking a break from parenting* and being less present and controlling in our children's lives, is a tool to help escape the narcissistic parenting that Jennifer Senior wrote about. The parent is *not so all-centrally-important to their child's life* that they must be present for every moment. You don't need to be involved in everything. Don't sweat the small stuff. Give yourself a break, lean back, and just breathe for a moment. You have other things in life that need tending to. Your child's happiness, success, and safety does not depend on your constant presence.

We can stop hovering and cede space back to children.

Young children, at home and at school, do not always need an activity – they can do absolutely "nothing" (from an adult perspective) for a long time and be perfectly content with it. We can intentionally leave space in their life that we do not fill with expectations, goals, or stimulation:

> *Noah's Note, March 2019:* I hope your kids are bored. And I hope you're not doing anything about it.
>
> Jennifer Senior reported in 2015 that in middle- and upper-class families, "each individual child, in our culture of fearful and controlling parenting, is subject to constant attention, vigilance, supervision, surveillance." Contrast that with Annette Lareau's research that in families where parents DID NOT invest themselves in their

children's play, children "tended to show more creativity, spontaneity, enjoyment, and initiative in their leisure pastimes" compared to children whose parents were heavily invested in their play and leisure activities.

Our children do not always have to be accomplishing something. Whimsy is good! Boredom is healthy! And, significantly for our own stress levels, we as parents need some hands-off time as well.

Parents and teachers can give children a transition-free and expectation-free space, removing the burden of always having somewhere to go and something to do. The default is to be busy, to be moving, to be *doing* something. Instead, we can actively curate a "bored" environment for our child:

Noah's Note, November 2023: Give your child long stretches without transitions. Got a free weekend morning? Do nothing and do it with your child. Loiter around the living room for hours together, building and smashing magnatiles, folding and putting away laundry, eating snacks and then getting more. Transitions are hard, right? So, eliminate the ones you don't need. Skip the park, skip the birthday party, skip the enrichment class. Let your child settle. Life should not be this fast paced. It is not good for us and certainly not for our children. The developing body, brain, and soul need time to chill.

Young children's lives are overscheduled and overstimulated. Stretch the length of time your child spends at home with nothing specific to do, no expectations to hit. Saturday mornings can be for pajamas and cereal followed by...nothing. Children in pre-school during the week have such a furious pace of transitions and scheduled activities. It is a real treasure for a young child to wake up one morning and find that nobody is asking them to be somewhere or to do something. This is where parents can serve as the child's ally instead of instructor: "There's a lot we need to get done today. But I can tell you've had an awfully busy week – we left home at 8am every day and barely got home by dinner each night. So how about we just chill at home this morning. I see you. Stay in your pajamas. I'll leave a bowl of fruit out. I think we'll really enjoy just hanging around."

And at school, we can leave blank space in our day – absent of any scripted activities or targeted curricula. We can acknowledge that it is OK, even desirable at times, for a child to sit by themselves or with others and not be engaged in an activity. Our burden does not need to be constant stimulation. These quiet moments give children the chance to breathe for a bit and sift through the busyness of the day. Teachers do not need to provoke children into participating in the activity or pepper them with questions and ideas. We can peel back and give space and time for children to be idle.

Let the quiet moments stay quiet.

Transitions at Home

It doesn't always have to be a fight!

Parents tend to enter the room with an agenda, with something they need to make happen – it's time to leave, it's time for bath, it's time for dinner. Our imperialism leads us to bark out the agenda before considering what the child is doing. Before interrupting your child, pause, take a breath, watch them, and consider: What are they doing? Are they focused and engaged? Do I need to interrupt them right now, to remind them to finish their cereal or blow their nose? Is it more important than what they're already doing? That little thing they're doing – scribbling, block building, doll playing – is their Neverland. It is meaningless to *us* but quite meaningful to *them*. Slide up next to them. Ogle at their painting or block structure or doll-figures. And *then* let them know what you needed to tell them. It means the world to a child to have an adult pause, see, and appreciate their activity before barking out a command or directive.

Parents can introduce "when you're ready" as a helpful time-oriented phrase in this moment, ceding *absolute* control to create a moment of mutuality. Instead of always insisting that the child complies with our timing, and then seeing their resistance as deviant, every so often we can just slow down instead of responding with strategies of control (bribing them to leave the house or punishing them if they don't). This leans into Deci and Ryan's "autonomy-supportive" stance, giving children autonomy over timed transitions rather than forcing them into immediate compliance. "We're leaving in five more minutes" turns into "I love the painting you're working on. And, I am ready to leave and will be at the front door. *When you're ready*, please get your shoes on and meet me there." Then try saying this if you can really mean it: "We are not in a rush. Just finish what you're doing and then come on over." This is an absolute gift for a young child – to hear that they don't need to finish their activity, right now and immediately, but that they have the grace of finishing on their own accord. This allows them, as Dr. Becky said, to *gaze in*. This can be shifted of course depending on urgency of timing: "This is your final activity – after you are finished using the blue crayon, meet me at the door." Each of these formulations allows the child to retain *some* autonomy in the transition while still maintaining that leaving the house is the next step.

And yes, of course, when leaving the house, very often there is just too great of a rush to slow down and do this. There are things that you need to be on time to. Then, there are many that you don't. It is ok to be late to the birthday party or soccer practice or playdate – or school! – because your child was in the middle of something and wasn't ready to leave. "When you're ready" removes so much of the power struggle – the battle for control – and still leaves the child plenty of incentive and motivation to wrap up what they're doing and join you. They want to be with you, they want to participate, they just don't want to be rushed and commanded. The parent here must be prepared to wait just a bit longer and be just a bit more patient (I know, a tall order!) but the yield is a child who gazes in (*"I am ready now"*) before gazing out (*"My parent needs me to be ready now"*). This does not need to be an every-time, or even an everyday, practice. Just try sprinkling it in, every so often, when you have the extra 2 minutes.

We can promote agency over compliance. Control does not need to be the guiding orientation in each moment. We can have symmetry in the relationship, if just for the moment. When we are both ready, we will leave.

Transitions at School

Preschool teachers can discard their timed schedules in favor of forming sensitive, responsive relationships with their students. This is a massive but simple shift – prioritize the relationship over the schedule:

◆ Transitions from one activity to the next can be made in small groups if needed, instead of insisting that everyone does everything at the same time.

◆ Snack can be made available *during* play time in the morning, out at a table for children to come to when hungry, instead of only when the teachers determine that play time is over. Food can be eaten by the child when they are hungry, not when the teacher tells them to eat.

◆ The first few children ready for the playground can leave with one teacher, while the other teacher lingers with those not yet finished playing or eating.

◆ Morning meeting can begin even while some children are busy elsewhere (like Zoe at the easel). Not all bodies need the same thing at the same time. This also leaves Zoe with a choice - the singing at morning meeting might entice her to come over on her own accord rather than at the request of a teacher. Small changes can have a big impact.

◆ During lunch, children can be allowed to leave the table to explore the classroom. They will return if hungry. If not, they don't need to be held captive at the table just because of what the schedule says.

◆ Play time can stretch until the children are ready to move on instead of at a predetermined time. I generally find that a preschool class needs at least 1 hour of completely un-interrupted free play each day, and often much more.

◆ Fewer scheduled "specials" or "enrichments" allow for more flexible transitions. In nearly every preschool class-room, play time ends because the teachers need to hurry the children on to the next activity, not because the children have exhausted their ideas, creativity, or explorations.

We can trust that children's internal clocks are better gauges of what they need than our printed schedules. This can all be boiled down into one simple maxim – *don't interrupt children.* Your idea of what they should do next is no more valuable or salient than *their* idea, especially if they are already engaged and focused on whatever task is at hand.

Alison Clark offers a meaningful meditation on "clock time" in early childhood in her 2023 book, *Slow Knowledge and the Unhurried Child: Time for Slow Pedagogies in Early Childhood Education* (*teachers, read this book!*). Clark weaves together astute observations and insights from academics and theorists along with first-person perspectives from on-the-ground early childhood educators about how time, schedules, and the clock have come to exert enormous pressure on the pace of the day and the resulting overall experience of the preschool classroom. She advocates for "a less hurried approach" (p. 44) in order to be more attentive to children's curiosities, questions, and concerns. Teachers can pay less attention to the clock and more attention to what children are doing. I don't think it is that preposterous for children to have the time they need, instead of the time we allocate. Clark's book is now on the syllabus for my doctoral course – she offers the right challenge to break preschool teachers out of their assumptions and habits about time and the use of the clock.

Claudia and I tried this out in our two-year-old classroom. We stopped following the timed schedule and instead followed the children. We played until we were done. We ate when the children were hungry. We went outside when they needed more space than our little classroom. We kept our parents in the loop, again through our Daily Emails:

January 19: We've been "flowing" as a class for the past few days - adjusting our schedule as needed based on the mood, energy, weather, etc. Today we had a longer than normal free play, from drop off [at 9:00am] until 10:30am. [Contrast this with my textbook at Fordham which had 45 minutes as the longest uninterrupted period in the preschool child's day.]

January 26: The play was so focused, engaged, and driven that we were able to again extend the length of our free play period (and cut down on transitions again), not stopping for snack until around 10:45. We cleaned up and by then it was too late to go out for our hike, so we went to the playground instead before heading back inside for lunch.

March 30: Everybody was vibing nicely with each other today. We began with a lengthy, extended period of free play - from 9:00 straight until snack at 10:30. We have recently dropped morning meeting, as the children dive right into play and no longer need the orientation to the day that meeting provides.

We found that our transitions were so much smoother – with no sheriffs, there were no outlaws. The children's agency came out as productive creativity instead of disruptive resistance. It was liberating not only for the children but for us as teachers as well.

Listening during Play

Play is a major vehicle for a child's learning, growth, and development, which leaves parents and teachers typically pushing a learning-oriented approach into their play time with children. We are constantly instructing: reminding children of how to appropriately use toys and sneaking small instructional moments into play. This is well and good, but we can do it less. A lot less. Our adult control already fully saturates their life. Sometimes children just need us to be their ally when they play, not their teacher or supervisor. Our constant instructions are too much for the child as we attempt to squeeze the learning out of every single moment: do this with the trains. Watch what I do with this toy. Don't do that with the puzzle. See how this works? This goes like this. All this talking leads to very little listening, and very little room for the child's agency and expression.

We can cut down on the words we use during play time with children and find ways to listen instead. Keep in mind that in a "serve and return" relationship, it is the *child* who serves and the adult who returns. Try to stop serving and start returning: pay attention to what the child is doing and follow their lead, returning to them what they have served to you. Adults can keep this in mind during play time with young children by simply listening to what children say and do and *reflecting it back to them* instead of adopting an instructive, corrective stance.

Then there are many times during play that children simply don't need adults talking much at all. Our words just aren't always necessary and are often interrupting and distracting while the child plays. Small, simple expressions and gestures by adults go a long way here. We can share our excitement, interest, encouragement, confusion, or dismay all without saying anything. This leaves the space open for the child to take the lead, knowing that we are there and engaged but following, not leading. A few key lines by Virginia Axline in her 1947 book Play Therapy, a groundbreaking work that established the nascent field of play therapy around her newly developed practices, have stuck with me throughout this research: "The therapist accepts the child exactly as he is. The therapist does not attempt to direct the child's actions or conversations in any manner. The child leads the way; the therapist follows" (p. 73). The reader is reminded in the book's introduction that "although directed especially to psychologists, psychiatrists, and case workers, Play Therapy is an important and rewarding book for parents, teachers, and anyone who comes in contact with children." When play is valued only for its learning potential, we forget to just be quiet and follow the child. Replace Axline's "therapist" with "teacher" or "parent" and you'll have a healthy approach to listening to young children during play.

We can leave more space for the child to fill by peeling back. Here's what it might look like to listen during play:

◆ A child places a toy zebra in their magnatile construction and looks up at their adult. "You made a zoo! Let's get more animals" instead becomes "I notice you put your zebra in your tower. I wonder what you'll do next!" Recognize *their idea* instead of labeling it or extending it.

◆ A child uses one brush to smush all the paint colors together and shows the painting to their adult. "I wish you hadn't done that, it ruins the paints" instead becomes "Wow, you mixed all the paint together! Let's look at what happened." Explore *their activity* with them instead of correcting it.

◆ A child gently rocks their baby doll and tells their adult, "My baby is crying, she misses her mommy." "Mommies come back, they always come back" instead becomes "Your baby is crying. She misses her mommy." Just like adults, children don't always need the solution presented to them – sometimes they just want to sit in the emotion. Reflect back *their emotions* instead of showing them how to move forward.

◆ A child tries and fails a few times at making a bridge out of blocks. They finally are successful, placing a long block to connect two columns. They look up at their adult. Loud, verbal celebrations by the adult instead become a gentle head nod and thin smile. They've worked hard because it is *their idea* not because they need your external validation.

We can build reciprocity and trust with our children when we show them that we are interested in *what they are doing* and not (always and only) telling them *what to do*. We can help them gaze in by not always asking them to gaze out. When we back off during play time and let children explore rather than offer instructions and "supposed to"s, children are capable of producing remarkable innovation and showcasing their desires for the world. Adults, less so – we are stuck in our ways, slower to experiment, and more prone to using things how they are meant to be used. Gopnik describes this succinctly as she reviews her clinical research into how children use materials in novel ways: "Grown-ups stick with the tried-and-true; four-year-olds have the luxury of looking for the weird and the wonderful" (2016, p. 104). This is where their Neverlands come from – their incessant desire and ability to conjure up newness, to add unexpected beauty to the world.

Just by sitting back and listening, we can welcome more of the weird and the wonderful into our world.

Listening to Emotions

When we see our children in distress, adults tend to default to talking instead of listening. We just can't help ourselves! We are so smart, so grownup, so *adult*, and what we do is talk. We explain things, over and over. We endlessly interrogate and push them to explain their feelings and behavior to us. We say one thing, and then we say it again, and again, and again. None of this creates an atmosphere conducive to listening to children; we generally just insist they listen to us.

We can shift this by re-orienting our expectations around verbal conversations with young children. Here are some approaches to listening to a young child during moments of emotional turbulence:

> *Noah's Note, September 2023: Children are either "ready" or "avoidant"*: A child will avoid talking about a difficult subject if they aren't ready, regardless of how well you phrase the question (or sweeten the pot with a bribe). If your child isn't ready to answer, "What's wrong, sweetie?", it's not helpful to keep asking it. But once your child is ready, watch out for a sudden outpouring of emotional statements. They will be ready on their own timeline, almost never on yours. Argh!
>
> *Engage them where they are*: This often means within playful fantasy, a role-playing scenario. It is said that "a child's playing it out is akin to an adult's talking it out." In a tough moment, you or I might sit with a dear friend or close partner and talk it out over a glass of wine or cup of coffee. For the young child, they need to play around with the subject matter. Both because it's the "language" they are most familiar with (what does your child do more: play, or converse?) but also because it affords them psychological distance: The person I am pretending to be is the one who is having a hard time, it's not actually ME. You might find success here by adding in figures – dolls, DUPLO people, even just odds & ends (corks make great fantasy people for kids – draw little faces on them!).

"This little boy is getting ready to go to school. His mommy will take him" – it's an invitation to play, but really an invitation to emotionally engage and process and listen to the child's response: "He is not ready to go to school! He will stay home with his mommy."

Reflect back, don't interrogate: Children can sniff out a detective and they clam up right away. Don't ask any questions. Just engage in the playful scenario, and when they're ready, it will tumble out. Follow their lead, reflect that you are listening (head nod, "mm-hmm"), show them their statements carry worth, and that you are here as their play (processing) partner. Follow, don't lead.

We can meet children where they are by saying less and listening more. This respects the child's space in the relationship, honoring them as a human with varying emotional states and needs, instead of painting them as a problem that the adult must conquer and solve. This shifts our stance away from attempting to get the child *out of* their big emotional state and toward meeting the child *within* their big emotional state. For a child crying or screaming, we can move away from "What do you need from me to stop?" or "Here, I have a sticker for you [or a prize, a snack, a treat]" and toward "I can tell you are having really big emotions right now. It must be so hard. I'm here for you." Children often have lots and lots of really messy, big emotions. They are complex. We need to listen to these emotions instead of solving for them or tricking our children out of them with distractions (screens, snacks, toys).

Do less solving and more listening.

Listening at School

We can build meaningful preschool curriculum by using a "pedagogy of listening" (Rinaldi, 2006). In a Reggio-inspired framework, this is referred to as an "emergent curriculum", as in, the curricular focus *emerges from* children's ideas, questions, and passions. This takes listening. Just like with Janie's pocket curriculum, the things children do can come to take over and re-define the class-room. Teachers can listen to children, observe their actions, and reflect them back to the class. This is a total departure from a scripted curriculum in which the teacher enters the year already knowing the activities. Instead, an emergent curriculum is like a winding river, often hard to see past the next bend, but always moving. There is an initial spark that sets it off – a great question or comment or bold action by a child (Janie's "I have a pocket"), and the accompanied recognition by the teacher that this moment matters. The children in this curriculum-as-river simile are the water – the vital lifeforce that gives the river power, energy, and meaning. The teachers are the banks of the river – without them the river dissipates in all directions, lacking trajectory or coherence. But the water always forces the issue and dictates the course that the river will run. Never in a straight line, never quite predictable. Resonant with Stetsenko's Transformative Activist Stance, the curriculum is co-constructed by the children and the teachers (like the banks of a river come together with the water to create the river).

In a classroom in my school a number of years ago, one child mentioned that they had been to a bowling alley over the weekend. A clamor arose from the children and they excitedly shared similar stories or asked questions. The teachers grabbed a pen and started writing it all down. The next morning, they recited the conversation back to the children. They told them that they heard how excited everyone was about bowling alleys and so they would begin to explore the topic as a class. Ilana – my preschool director when I became a teacher – had told me early on that in a Reggio-inspired classroom, if you saw a child petting a dog, your job was to determine what it was that the child was actually interested in. Was it the dog? Or the physical sensation of feeling the dog's bony spine and prickly fur? Or the emotions of caring for another living being? Or the relational memories of visiting a grandparent who had a dog at their house? The teacher has to really, really get down to the child's level, drop their assumptions about what the curriculum is supposed to be about, or what the teacher wants the curriculum to be about, and listen to the child. So, the bowling alley curriculum began from that spark but then took off in all sorts of directions as the teachers listened to the students and the river meandered. The curriculum began in October and stretched all the way to May because it mattered to the children – it was *theirs*.

During an initial flurry of children playing "bowling alley", the teachers wrote down what they heard and observed and, again, reflected this back to children. The children wanted to go to the bowling alley and now were busy figuring out how to get there, so the curriculum shifted into maps and navigating. They spent a long time pouring over subway maps and bus routes, figuring out how to get from school to the bowling alley. Then the teachers realized the children were clamoring over the rules of bowling, as they all disagreed on how to actually bowl. The curriculum shifted again and focused on games with rules – all sorts of games and how to play them; they even started making up their own games with their own rules. The music teacher was in on our curricular approach and pulled the ideas into his weekly sessions with the class. They wrote a song for the bowling alley, with the chorus, "Bowling pins are falling down/It sounds like ice is falling from the sky/We push the ball round and round/ The pins fall down on their side." After their successful field trip, they realized the real bowling alley had a name and a sign, which they wanted for their classroom too. After much deliberation and disagreement, they settled on "Classroom 4 World Bowling Alley." A group of students spent a long time scratching out the shaky letters of a young writer to create the sign. They created their own bowling alley in the classroom, spending weeks hashing out the details of balls, pins, bumpers, friction, turn-taking, and scorekeeping.

A critical listening tool for teachers as they develop an emergent curriculum is a notebook and pen. This allows teachers to jot down observations of what the children are playing, doing, and saying – all those emergent Neverlands – instead of always talking and teaching. The key here is that these observations are not (only) developmental notes, assessing where children are meeting their milestones and where they are struggling. They are also used to reflect back to the children (as I did with Janie and the teachers did with the bowling alley) what we've noticed they are doing, invite others to join, and offer embellishments or extensions of the activity. Consider what might have happened if this was done with Emily's attempt at peekaboo in the bathroom. Instead of banning the activity, the teachers could have foregrounded it during morning meeting, bringing Emily's contagious excitement to the class and allowing her to take the lead in building a curriculum around the game. Listening can turn a child from an outlaw into a leader.

Notebooks are used not only to record the children's voices but to amplify them: they are the tool of an ally. The class curriculum then stems forth from the notebook, filled with children's ideas, passions, and questions, rather than the teachers' or curriculum developers' assumptions about what children that age like to do or should spend their time doing. This is a small act with a big impact. I describe this to teachers as a megaphone – using a notebook to write down children's thoughts is like handing the child a megaphone. The effect is contagious, as children recognize they are being listened to and start voicing their ideas more freely. A four-year-old came up to me once while I was taking notes while watching free play and tapped me on the shoulder. She wanted to make sure I heard what she said: "Noah, did you write that down?" She knew that her actions mattered. All it takes is listening instead of teaching. Teachers can use their notebooks at morning meeting to help set the stage for the day. "Here's what we're going to play today" turns into "Here's what I heard some of you playing yesterday, and here's how we can extend that play today."

Involve More: Access, Participation, and Contribution

Young children can do real things, with real things.

They can serve as apprentices to just about everything that adults do, contributing productively through legitimate peripheral participation. There are a few obvious exceptions such as sexual intimacy, consumption of illicit substances, and acts of violence; I would add digital media consumption but believe that is less "obvious" and more personal. Outside of those, I see few-to-zero parts of normal, daily life that children really have to be kept out of. Young children can acquire technical skills that *are actually useful* by being involved in the production processes at home and at school, where they can learn craftsmanship and tool use from those with more experience. But *children must be part of the world* in order to do this, which means being freed from the constraints of age-based segregation and its infantilizing effects. Children need to be re-introduced to the world! This re-introduction can be oriented around what is relevant to their livelihood instead of only what is assumed about their age. They need access to, and participation with, the daily life of the world around them instead of only the narrow world of early childhood textbooks. Young children, when given access, can comfortably participate in daily household tasks, simple tool use, common craft materials, commerce, culture, transportation – the general, basic, repetitive things around them. When this topic comes up in my weekly Coffee Chats, I routinely hear from parents that their child is *proud* to be able to contribute to the house, by making their own bed or feeding the dog.

These are not discrete tasks but are part of a broad pattern of cultural participation that is fully absent in an imperial childhood. It's not just a simple checklist of things but a stance toward the world: *participation* can replace *resistance* as the way in which children meet their world. These are not banal chores: they are chances for children to matter, to be a part of something meaningful. Nobody likes being useless. Children can:

◆ Use, alongside an adult, common tools such as a hammer, screwdriver, saw, and shovel. Children can master these tools and then use them proficiently and independently through access and participation, not only biological growth and development.

◆ Participate in, and eventually do on their own, routine household processes like preparing food, doing the laundry, cleaning the dishes, taking out the garbage, and sweeping the floor.

◆ Comprehend large cultural systems such as commerce and transportation through their participation within the daily routines of those systems, such as purchasing groceries and traveling on the bus.

Ten-year-olds can't do laundry not because they're biologically inept but because their *sociocultural development* prevented
them from participating in the act as a young child. This is the
earliest point in the journey that Lythcott-Haims described as
ending in the "cliff" of independence. She talked about college
students showing up on campus not knowing how to do their own
laundry (or anything, really). Where do you think that started?
When they were two and three years old and their adult put their
dirty laundry in the hamper for them every night. Recall Lave,
"We are always learning what we are already doing." When we
don't "do" laundry we don't learn it.

A lot of this comes from modifying access to materials and
resources, which allows children to then participate and eventually contribute. I've come to think about children's access
to resources along the same lines of ADA (the Americans
with Disabilities Act) – when we are responsible for an environment, it is our responsibility to ensure that *all* community
members have reliable ways to access the things they need. Just
like a ramp allows a person who uses a wheelchair to access a
building, modified access around the house or classroom allows
a child to get what they need as they go about their daily life.
For example, why don't all preschools have a child-height railing
on staircases? The lack of access to the railing delays the age at
which children can competently descend a staircase. We place a
handrail for when adults need support but we hoist our children
up instead of providing them access to the same support.

Access leads to participation which leads to contribution. By
participate, I mean "join in" and by *contribute*, I mean "be productive" but also contribute to the shaping of the activity itself.
This is where Stetsenko's Transformative Activist Stance tells
us that children are not static receivers of mature community
activities – they will add in their own novel ways that modify the
activity and, additionally, shift our behavior with their presence.
This is why, and how, cultural practices are modified from generation to generation. As humans, we receive culture *and also contribute to changing it* all at the same time (we have agency!). The
things that we do change when we do them with children. As
Gopnik writes, "Each new generation of children is a shot of noise,

a little dose of disorder, shaking up the stable patterns of previous generations and allowing for new possibilities" (2016, p. 35).

Using "contribute" in this sense, we could say that Emily *contributed to the practice of throwing a ball* when she taught me her own version of catch. In the same way, Emily ate her pancake down the middle, and her mango straight from the freezer – her own personal flair. This is how children contribute to reshaping our adult practices. A mother shared with me that her husband would make a "giant breakfast burrito" each morning but their five-year-old would eat some of it, so the father began making a "mini breakfast burrito" for her as well. Having children present in our practices changes those practices. It all begins with access and participation.

Finding an Entry Point

There is nearly always some small way for the child to participate in, and then contribute to, the task at hand. This just requires finding the right entry point for involvement and legitimate peripheral participation as early on as possible. The later you start, the harder that entry point becomes – both for the adult to provide and for the child to participate in.

Let's take a look at how to actually find the entry point to participation for young children at home:

- ◆ Very young children can put their dirty clothes in the hamper every time they change. Slightly older children can put their folded, clean clothes in their drawers. Children can match socks and learn to fold them together.
- ◆ Children can participate alongside an adult in putting clothes from the hamper in the washing machine, starting the cycle, and transferring them to the drying machine.
- ◆ Common kitchen items can be moved to a child's height so they can get their own dishes, silverware, and cups, as well as basic food items like cereal, fruit, and snacks. Again, this is not a chore for the child to do by themselves, but in tandem with an adult who is doing the same thing –

setting the table and preparing food. It is the *doing with* that makes this work. A child can get the cereal, bowl, and spoon, but the milk carton might be too heavy, so the adult does that. We work *together.*

◆ A stool can be used to bring the child up to counter height, where they can stay close to an adult and participate while cooking. They can pick up small tasks along the way like washing, pouring, mixing, stirring, measuring, tasting. Rinsing blueberries is an easy entry point here – something in the kitchen that a child can successfully do.

◆ Real utensils allow children to cut their own food and feed themselves more easily. Swap out plastic toddler utensils for the real deal once your child has the hang of it. Try using the smallest place settings, such as the salad fork and the coffee spoon. They can participate more in the basic acts of mealtime when given actual utensils. Try using a toddler knife to cut chicken or a toddler fork to spear a piece of salmon. It doesn't work.

◆ Small brooms, dustpans, and hand vacuums can be used by children to clean up messes alongside adults.

◆ Gardening and yardwork like watering, weeding, digging, and clipping can be done by children alongside their adults.

◆ Children can help prepare for the day at school by placing items in their school bag, such as a lunchbox, water bottle, and rain boots.

◆ Children can also help in assembling their school lunch – at first just placing items together in the lunchbox but, after enough participation, preparing the actual lunch food itself.

◆ Children can appropriately place items in the garbage, recycling, or compost.

◆ Children can participate in grocery shopping by selecting certain items, placing items in the shopping cart, crossing items off the list.

◆ Children can help prepare for the grocery store, together with an adult, by taking an inventory of the fridge and the pantry.

◆ Stools allow children to turn their light on and off.

♦ Children can use a small hammer or screwdriver to participate in repairs alongside an adult.

And a look at these entry points to access, participation, and contribution at school:

♦ Arts and crafts materials can be left out on a shelf at a child's height for them to use throughout the day: paper, scissors, tape, pencils, crayons, glue, stapler, hole puncher, paint. This allows children to take the materials they need instead of either only using the ones presented by the teachers or relying on requesting them from the teacher (which is often met with a "No, that's not for now"). Unimpeded access to these materials leads to children mastering how to use them which leads to easier and more competent participation in many daily activities.

♦ Teachers can prepare less on their own and do more with students. Elements of the classroom like "job charts" can be made as a class, collectively, instead of purchased or made ahead of time by the teachers. Rather than presenting these *to* our classroom, we can make them *with* our students. Children can contribute their novel ideas instead of relying on the same job chart used each year. A classroom in my New York school once had a "feelings helper" in their job chart because one child noticed another child was often crying at clean-up time.

♦ Students can participate in the preparation and distribution of snack and lunch food. Collecting items from the fridge, washing and chopping fruit, preparing the table, and passing out food are all things that children can do. Teachers and students can jointly share this work, with teachers modeling and doing the bulk of the task while students participate peripherally (in my DC school, we designed our kitchen island to have a long, two-tiered riser on one side, so that a whole class of students can access the adult-height island countertop and participate with adults). Leave lunchboxes in an accessible location in children's cubbies so they can retrieve it themselves when needed.

Small changes in access can lead to big changes in contributions. When we remove the hurdles in front of children (that we ourselves have created), we can recognize their strengths and capacities in a new way.

All by Themselves

There are so many times that parents and teachers do things for young children that the child can already do by themselves. For many of these things, our presence is distracting at best and debilitating at worst. It's complex and nuanced though so I'll break this down before moving forward.

Sometimes, we do this (*this* being *infantilize children when we do things for them that they can already do themselves*) because we are in a rush. I get it, and it's unavoidable. If you're in a rush, put the child's shoes on and stop badgering them to do it! They *can* put their shoes on. They *cannot* do it in a rush. Step in and get it done for them but try to mention along the way: "Honey, I'm in a bit of a rush this morning, so I'll just do your shoes for you" (noncontrolling, autonomy-supportive). Acknowledge their competency and reflect back that it's *you* who need this to happen quickly so it's *you* who will do it. Then there are the times we do it as an expression of love and compassion. I often hear from parents who carry their young child (who can walk) into preschool that they do this because they just love the snuggles and this is their chance each morning to have physical connection. I'm all for it, and again think it would pair nicely with an intentional reflection: "Sweetie, I know you are a strong girl who can walk all by herself. And I know we love snuggling every morning, so I'd love to carry you into school." There is a perhaps apocryphal story told of an American preschool teacher visiting the schools of Reggio Emilia, in Italy, who observes an Italian educator diligently buttoning up every single student's peacoat. The American notices the children are of an age that they can likely do this by themselves and asks the Italian educator, "Why are you doing all of that for them?" to which the Italian responds, "How else would they know I love them?" *Doing for others* can be an expression of love. All well and good.

And then there are other reasons we do things for our children that I believe we would do well to leave behind us: because we don't recognize our child's newfound strengths, because we are just in the habit of doing for them (like the mother who wrote to me, in Chapter 4, about "falling on habits"), because we just don't believe in our children's capacity. All of these reasons kind of coalesce around one core motivation to do things for our children – we want to retain control over the outcome. The lunch has to be set up the way *we* want it. The bow has to be in the hair the way *we* want it. It leaves us doing *everything* for our child despite their obvious capacity to be doing many (*many!*) of these things by themselves. Now, of course, children will always be dependent on their parents for different things at different times in their life – as humans, we will always need each other. But for young children, we do *far too much* for them because of the imperial prism that we see them through.

Standing with a father at a playground, we chatted and watched as his two-year-old scaled a climbing tower. "Whoa," the dad remarked to me, "I didn't know he could do that!" I had this in mind when sitting with a preschool teacher the following week. We were reviewing one child in her class and the teacher was frustrated because she believed the child's parents underestimated the child's competencies. The teacher exclaimed with passion, "It's like, I just want to tell them, 'Believe in your children!'" This is a pattern I see *all the time* – parents surprised to find out what their children are capable of, and teachers surprised that parents don't see their child's capabilities. Children need the adults in their lives to trust that they can do these things before they've proven it. When children attempt to do things we don't think they can do, we can back away and stand aside as they prove our assumptions wrong.

So, fittingly, this final chapter concludes with a (very partial, suggestive) list of things a young child can do by themselves, without an adult being involved, or even watching:

◆ Make a friend.
◆ Go up and down the slide.
◆ Climb tall elements on the playground.
◆ Navigate conflict resolution with a peer.

- ◆ Use paint.
- ◆ Crawl into nooks and crannies.
- ◆ Feed themselves.
- ◆ Fall down (even on hard surfaces!) and get back up.
- ◆ Build blocks, trains, and magnatiles.

References

Axline, V. (1947). *Play therapy*. Ballentine Books.

Clark, A. (2023). *Slow knowledge and the unhurried child: Time for slow pedagogies in early childhood education*. Routledge.

Gopnik, A. (2016). *The gardener and the carpenter: What the new science of child development tells us about the relationship between parents and children*. Farrar, Straus and Giroux.

Rinaldi, C. (2006). *In dialogue with Reggio Emilia: Listening, researching and learning*. Routledge, Taylor and Francis.

Rosin, H. *The Overprotected Kid*. The Atlantic, April 2014. https://www.theatlantic.com/magazine/archive/2014/04/hey-parents-leave-those-kids-alone/358631/

Epilogue

For me, this all works – this new relationship with children where control less and trust more, where we do less and involve more. It's taken me a minute to get this all sorted out, but it's an approach that I'm now comfortable with within my various roles in early childhood. But it took time, and it wasn't easy or always clear. I hope it works for you too and I hope it works for your child or your students. I hope you re-read the parts of the book you were frustrated with. I hope you come back to the book in six months, when a lightbulb goes off when watching your child or students play – *THIS is what he meant!* I find these ideas are best considered while engaged with our children and while watching them engage with the world. Their actions animate my ideas more than a book ever could.

But it might not work for you. Our lives are all different. Our relationships are all different. Our children are all different. My goal has been to present some prevailing cultural patterns in the way we relate to our children that are tweakable, allowing parents and teachers to critically reflect on changes they can make. Choose your own adventure here – find what works, discard what doesn't, and make it yours.

Me, I'm working on controlling less and trusting more, on believing in children – in their statements, in their capacities, in their dreams.

In preschool these days, I find myself looking less and less for teachable, educational moments and more for joyful, relational moments. Interacting with students, I'm thinking, *How can we connect?* rather than, *What can you learn?* Pockets, hot dogs, bowling alleys, paintings – children all have things that matter to them. I try to make them matter to me, too. I try to let myself be impacted by the child's actions. I try to squeal with glee when they show me that tiny treasure they found earlier and have held tightly, clutched in their warm, sweaty palm all day. I try to share in their delight. I pause more, a literal pause in motion, to stay in one place and watch the frenetic energy of preschoolers, so I can see, find, and feel their natural rhythm. I find that simply standing still and carefully watching is often a good choice.

As a parent, I find myself working on having a higher threshold for when I am needed by my children. I do my best to give them more time with their frustration, or struggle, or peer negotiation before I get involved. They can solve more on their own when I am less present. When they are engaged with something – anything – I try to interrupt them less and give them more time and space to do whatever it is they are doing – whether it's painting their masterpiece or rolling around the living room aimlessly. I find myself just staying quieter, generally, so that the children have more space to fill in. We're working on shifting the balance around the house away from us parents doing *everything* and the children doing *nothing* and toward everyone in the house participating together in keeping the house tidy and productive. Sometimes it works. Sometimes it doesn't. We're only human.

I e-mailed Zoe while finishing the book, sharing an early draft. Now finishing high school, she told me she still has the painting, 14 years later. She wrote back:

> I read the passage about me the night before my graduation while trying on my cap and gown.
>
> Thank you for letting me paint and express myself creatively. You as a teacher made a huge impact on me. Putting vulnerability and emotion in my work is something I have never been afraid to do. Making that butterfly painting and the support that you provided is something I have remembered.

What I've learned is that we all need each other. Zoe taught me to believe in children's power – she mattered to me. And I mattered to her – the support I offered in curating her space each morning and then backing off.

In a mutual, reciprocal relationship, we both matter.

That's all this is. Re-thinking how we relate so that we can acknowledge, accommodate, and embrace the ways in which each of us matters.

Acknowledgments

Emily, thank you for sharing your world with me. I pray that I have described your experiences faithfully and truthfully. Kate and John, thank you for welcoming me into your life for a year and allowing me unfettered access. Kate, thank you for your endless kindness and patience as I tagged along, always with more questions.

Tanya, Michelle, and Yasmin, thank you for allowing me into your classroom and always making me feel comfortable. The warmth and love you show your students is not captured here, as it is not the focus of my writing, but was plain and obvious in your classroom every day. I am so grateful you allowed me to do this work in your classroom.

Thank you to my JCC Manhattan family. Your support and inspiration carried me through all of this: Rabbi Joy Levitt, Dava Schub, Ilana Ruskay-Kidd, Felicia Gordon, Shari Pick-Taishoff, Tara Ekelman, Linda Sierra, Alex Reynolds, Jamie Schneider, Pamela Echtenkamp, Deb Wasserman, Mark Horowitz, and countless others.

Thank you to my Teachers College team, who guided me through the research process, always offering the right blend of critique, support, and insight: Dr. Susan Recchia, Dr. Haeny Yoon, Dr. Juliette de-Wolfe, Dr. Michelle Knight-Manuel, and Dr. Mariana Souto-Manning.

Dr. Anna Stetsenko, thank you for your profound generosity of spirit and intellectual passion. You helped bring my ideas to life and always pushed me to be bold. By the time we met, you had been in academics for a lifetime but never flinched at taking me under your wing just as I was getting started. I am eternally grateful.

Thank you to Darci Lewis, Stephanie Slater, and my Gan HaYeled Preschool family, who every day create and sustain a joyful, inclusive, antiracist, Reggio-inspired community for our youngest citizens. Jess Jones-Sills, thank you for engaging me throughout this process and helping to stretch and define my ideas as they settled. Thank you to the dozens and dozens of Gan teaching faculty for your grace and kindness as I've explored these ideas with you. You are each remarkable. I am delighted to be on this journey with you.

Thank you to my American Jewish University family, for taking me in and showing me what the next step in my journey looks like. Dr. Tamar Andrews, thank you for seeing something in me and giving me the space to work through some of these ideas with my students.

Thank you to the talented and passionate co-teachers I have had the pleasure of teaching alongside over the years. Many of the themes in this book first arose while spending my days with you. But most importantly, you allowed me to have fun in the classroom: Shannon, Hillary, Marlowe, Amanda, Tamar, Jen, Laurie, Vicki, and Claudia.

Thank you to my children's preschool teachers over the years. You are each an absolute rock star! My children carry you with them throughout their lives: Alex, Theresa, Lara, Carla, Joanie, Shira, Aida, Lindsey, Kendra, Lauren, Tate, Neidia, Diane, Ashley, Erin, Adelina, LaVonda, Matt, Kristen, and Berfaly.

Thank you to the Parkview Crew for creating a magical neighborhood where our children can run free, away from our prying adult eyes. Thank you to the Weekenders for giving us all a space to try out horizontal parenting. I know that our children are richer for the time we leave them alone, exploring the vastness of their own private Neverlands.

Index

For Product Safety Concerns and Information please contact our EU
representative GPSR@taylorandfrancis.com
Taylor & Francis Verlag GmbH, Kaufingerstraße 24, 80331 München, Germany